HOMESCIENCE EXAM COMPANION: VITAL QUESTIONS DECODED

TREESA SINDHU P. THOMAS & DR. LEENA LEON

Made with ♥ on the Notion Press Platform

www.notionpress.com

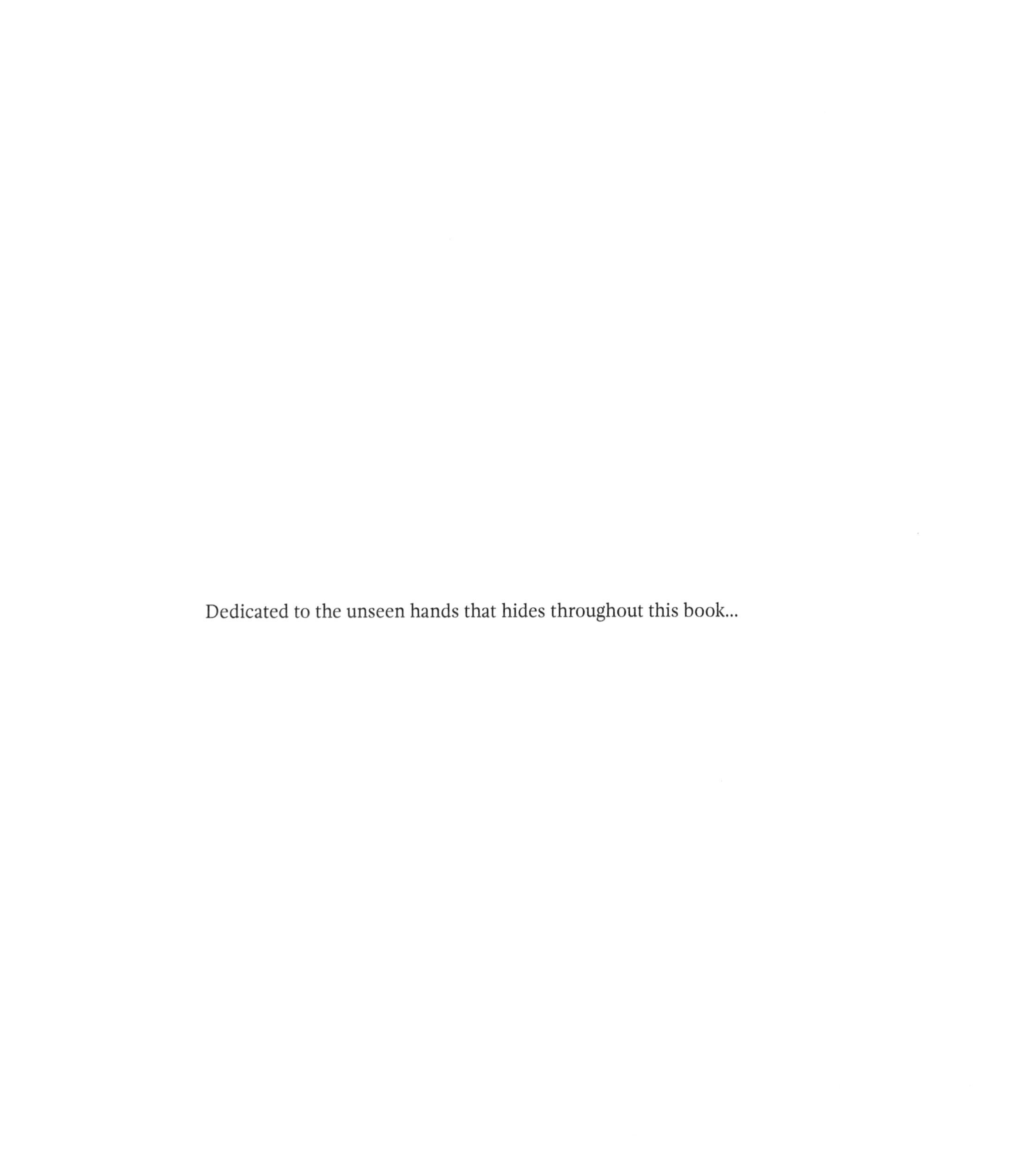

Dedicated to the unseen hands that hides throughout this book...

Contents

Preface

Welcome to "Home Science Exam Companion: Vital Questions Decoded." As students embark on their journey through the fascinating world of Home Science, we are delighted to present this comprehensive question bank tailored specifically for students of the XI Home Science based on state syllabus and strictly adhered to the SCERT textbook.

This book has been meticulously crafted with one goal in mind: to serve as a reliable companion for students preparing for their plus one Home Science examinations. Drawing from the SCERT textbook, we have curated a collection of important and repeat questions along with their detailed answers, ensuring comprehensive coverage of the curriculum.

Understanding the importance of clarity and simplicity in learning, we have designed this book in a manner that is easy to read and comprehend. Each answer is presented in a straightforward and concise manner, making it accessible to students of all levels. With this resource at hand, students can navigate through complex topics with confidence and clarity.

Our aim is to provide students with a valuable tool that not only aids in exam preparation but also enhances their understanding of Home Science concepts. By decoding vital questions and presenting them in an accessible format, we hope to empower students to excel in their examinations and beyond.

We extend our sincere gratitude to the educators and experts who have contributed to the creation of this book, ensuring its accuracy and relevance to the curriculum. We also express our appreciation to the students whose dedication and commitment to learning continue to inspire us.

As students delve into the pages of "Home Science Exam Companion: Vital Questions Decoded," may they find clarity, confidence, and success in their academic pursuits.

Authors

CHAPTER I

Home Science: Concept and Scope

1. If behavioural problems of children: Human development

Time management: --------------------

Audio Visual Aids: ---------------------

Ans. Family and Community Resource Management, Extension Education

2. Applied nutrition and basis of programme planning are included under ------ area of Home Science.

Ans. Extension education

3. Area of Home Science which deals with consumer problems and education.

Ans. Family and Community Resource Management

4. Name the area of Home Science related with preparation of audio visual aids and method of communication.

Ans. Extension education

5. Expand a) FAO b) CARE c) UNICEF

Ans. a) Food and Agricultural Organisation

b) Cooperative for American Relief Everywhere

c) United Nations International Children's Emergency Fund

6. List the major areas of home science.

Ans. The major areas of home science are:

a) Human Development

b) Family and Community Resource Management

c) Food and Nutrition

d) Textile Science

e) Extension Education

7. Name the area of Home Science dealing with the study of behavioural problems of children.

Ans. Human Development

8. Name the area of Home Science subject related to the study of fibres and fabrics, apparel designing and construction.

Ans. Textile Science

9. Identify the area of Home Science where Geriatrics is a part of the study.

a) Extension education, b) Human Development, c)Textile Science, d) Family and community Resource Management

Ans. Human Development

10. Choose the correct expansion of FAO from the following:

a) Food Authority Organization, b) Fruit and Agricultural Organisation, c)Food and Agricultural Organization

Ans. Food and Agricultural Organization

11. Find the area of Home Science which covers the study of consumer education, principles and basics of design. Human development, Textile science, Family and Resource Management

Ans. Family and Resource Management

12. Identify the area of Home Science in which the study of chemistry of food, nutritive value of food, etc. are included.

a)Human Development b)Textile Science c)Food and Nutrition d)Extension Education Ans. c) Food and Nutrition

13. Name the area of Home Science which includes the study of development of a child from conception to old age.

a)Food and Nutrition b)Textile Science c)Human Development d)Extension Education Ans. c) Human Development

14. Find the area of Home Science dealing with basics of programme planning and preparation of audio visual aids.

Ans. Extension Education

****

CHAPTER II

Introduction to Human Development

1. Find out the suitable hereditary disorder from the description given below.

a) Uric acid build up in the joints ------------------ (Gout)

b) Red blood cells become sickle shaped----------------(Sickle cell anaemia)

c) High blood glucose level ----------------------- (Diabetes)

d) Blood does not clot -------------------(Haemophilia)

e) Muscle weakness and muscle loss -------------- (Muscular Dystrophy)

f) Presence of extra chromosomal material---------- (Down Syndrome)

g) Blurred distant vision and clear nearer vision ------ (Myopia)

2. Select the odd one.

Sickle cell anaemia, Muscular dystrophy, Malnutrition, Myopia

Ans. c) Malnutrition

3. Implantation in the uterine wall is related with which of the following pre-natal stage?

a) Period of foetus b) Period of embryo c) Period of ovum, d) None of the above

Ans. c) Period of ovum

4. There is a condition in which blood does not clot normally and this results in severe bleeding from minor wounds. Identify the disease.

Ans. Haemophilia

5. Name the hereditary disorder in which an extra chromosomal material on pair number 21, which causes mental retardation and distinct physical features.

Ans. Down's syndrome

6. If ability to communicate : Language development,

Ability to solve problems : ----------------------

Ans. Cognitive development

7. Analyse the following examples and find out the corresponding principles of growth and development.

a) Children of tall parents are generally tall.

b) Disappearance of baby hair and baby teeth.

c) The heart, liver and digestive organs grow slowly in childhood, but rapidly during the early years of adolescence.

Ans. a) Development is predictable.

b)Development involves changes.

c)Different areas develop at different rates.

8. Hurlock defines ----------------- as a progressive series of orderly coherent changes.

Ans. Development

9. Find the odd one out from the following:

a) Period of ovum, b) Period of embryo, c) Period of infancy, d)Period of foetus

Ans. c) Period of infancy

10. Odd one out.

a) Period of ovum b)Period of embryo c)Period of foetus d) Period of infancy

Ans. Period of infancy

11. 'A child can hold his head only after neck muscles are strong enough to hold it'. Identify the principles of growth and development.

Ans. Development is due to maturation

12. Identify the principles of growth and development from the following examples:

a) Disappearance of old features and acquisition of new features.

b) The heart, liver and the digestive organs grow slowly in childhood, but rapidly during the early years of adolescence.

Ans. a) Development involves changes

b) Different areas develop at different rates

2 Mark Questions and Answers

13. Define Growth and Development

As we grow, our bodies undergo physical changes that make us bigger and stronger and longer. Meanwhile, development refers to the combination of both qualitative and quantitative changes over time. According to Hurlock (2011), this process involves a series of gradual and consistent transformations.

14. Write a short note on Gout.

Ans. Gout occurs when there is an accumulation (buildup) of uric acid in the bloodstream. Uric acid is a byproduct that is created in the body on a daily basis and expelled through the kidneys. If the body produces an excessive amount of uric acid or if not enough is eliminated during urination, the uric acid can accumulate and lead to the development of small crystals that cause discomfort and inflammation in and around the joints.

15. Write short notes on sickle cell anaemia and haemophilia.

Ans. a) Sickle Cell Anaemia: It is a genetic condition where red blood cells are malformed, causing them to take on a sickle shape instead of their normal rounded or doughnut shape. This can hinder the cells' ability to carry oxygen throughout the body, leading to anemia when the misshapen cells block small blood vessels.

b) Haemophilia: Haemophilia is a medical condition that causes blood to not clot properly, leading to excessive bleeding from even small cuts. It can be life-threatening if not managed properly. While this disorder primarily impacts males, females can be carriers of the gene.

16. Development involves changes. Justify.

Ans. The major changes involved are:

a) **Change in size**: The height and weight of the body changes with progression in time.

b) **Change in proportion**: As the size of the body increased, body proportion is also increased.

17.Development is sequential. Justify.

Ans. In human development, there is a set order that is followed. There are two main sequences that can be observed. Firstly, development starts from the head and moves down to the toes (Cephalo-caudal). For example, a child learns to control their head first, then their trunk, and eventually their legs. Secondly, development occurs from the center of the body outwards (proximo-distal). For instance, a child may first catch a ball using both arms, then with their palms, and finally with their fingers.

4 Mark Questions and Answers

18. Differentiate between Growth and Development.

Ans.

Growth

Increase in size, height and weight of the body.

Can be measured and observed

It is limited. Starts with birth to maturity

Limited to specific areas

Quantitative change

Development

Overall development and improvement in the functioning of the body process

Cannot be measured easily

A continuous unending process till death

Concerned with various aspects and parts of body and behaviour as a whole

Qualitative as well as Quantitative change

19. Age Span for the Human developmental Stages-Post-natal Period

Stages Age Period

Infancy - From birth to two years

Childhood - From the 3 to 12 years

Early Childhood - From 3 to 6 years

Late Childhood - From 7 to12 years or puberty

Adolescence - From 13 to 19 years

Adulthood - From 20 to 60 years

Oldage - From 61 years till death

20. Describe the important areas of development

Physical Development - changes in height and weight and changes in size and shape of the body

Motor Development - Development of control over bodily movements through the co-ordinated activity of the nerve centres, the nerves and the muscles.

Language and Speech Development - Development of any form of language (gestures, emotional expressions, speech or written language)

Emotional Development - Development of the ability to express, control, understand and accept one's emotions

Social Development - Acquisition of the ability to behave in accordance with social expectations.

Cognitive/ Intellectual Development - Helps a person to memorize, imagine, communicate, perceive and to solve problems.

21. Give an account of any three factors affecting growth and development.

Ans. a) Sex: Gender plays a role in the growth and development of individuals, with boys typically being taller and more daring than girls. Girls experience a rapid growth spurt during adolescence.

b) Nutrition: Proper nutrition is crucial for a child's growth and development, affecting both physical and mental well-being. Inadequate diet during growth stages can lead to various deficiencies and stunt growth.

c) The hormones produced by internal glands, such as the thyroid gland, are essential for physical and mental development. Hormonal balance also influences the development of masculinity in individuals.

22. Prepare a short note on any three areas of human development.

Ans. a) Physical development: Which entails the growth in height and weight, resulting in alterations in the body's size and shape.

b) Motor development: It involves gaining control over bodily movements through the coordinated actions of nerve centers, nerves, and muscles.

c) Language and speech development: It is crucial for effectively expressing thoughts and emotions through communication. It involves the capacity to use meaningful words to convey messages to others and comprehend the meanings of words spoken by others.

23. Discriminate the role of heredity and environment in growth and development.

Ans. Heredity is the process where physical and social traits pass from parents to offspring, influencing growth and development like height, weight, body structure, hair and eye color, intelligence, and aptitude. It includes all traits present in an individual at birth.

Environment refers to factors that impact an organism besides heredity from conception onwards. There are three types of environment: physical, social, and psychological. The physical environment includes food, clothing, shelter, weather, and climate. The social environment includes society, individuals, and institutions.

6 Mark questions and answers

24. Describe the principles of growth and development

* **Development involves changes** - "Significant changes in the body as a child grows include increasing size, changes in proportion, the loss of old features, and the development of new features. As a child grows, their height and weight increase each year. Additionally, the proportion of certain body parts changes. For example, at birth, the head makes up one-fourth of the body length, but in adulthood, it only accounts for one-eighth. Some old features, such as milk teeth and baby hair, disappear or change as the child grows. At the same time, new features like permanent teeth and the emergence of primary and secondary characteristics are acquired."

***Development is predictable** – Every person is special in their own way, but the growth rate of each child tends to be fairly consistent. We can somewhat forecast how quickly a child will develop. For example, kids with tall parents usually end up being tall themselves.

***Development is sequential** - In human development, there is a set order that is followed. There are two main sequences that can be observed. Firstly, development starts from the head and moves down to the toes (Cephalo-caudal). For example, a child learns to control their head first, then their trunk, and eventually their legs. Secondly, development occurs from the center of the body outwards (proximo-distal). For instance, a child may first catch a ball using both arms, then with their palms, and finally with their fingers.

***Development proceeds from general to specific responses** - In the beginning, babies' reactions are quite broad, but as they grow older, they become more focused. For example, when kids are first learning to speak, they might say 'toy' before they learn the names of individual toys.

25. Differentiate various hereditary disorders.

Ans. **Haemophilia:** Haemophilia is a disorder where the blood doesn't clot properly, causing excessive bleeding from small injuries. It typically impacts males, while females are carriers.

b) **Muscular Dystrophy:** Muscular dystrophy refers to a collection of over 30 genetic conditions that result in weakness and atrophy of the muscles.

c) **Down's Syndrome:** Down Syndrome is a genetic condition caused by an extra chromosome on pair 21, leading to cognitive delays and unique physical characteristics such as almond-shaped eyes and flat facial features.

d) **Phenyl-Ketonuria:** Phenylketonuria is a metabolic disorder that affects the body's ability to properly break down phenylalanine, an amino acid found in milk and high-protein foods like meat. When the liver is unable to metabolize phenylalanine, it and other metabolic byproducts build up in the blood, leading to a lack of nutrients in the nervous system and ultimately causing severe mental retardation.

e) **Diabetes:** Diabetes is a condition where a person has high blood sugar due to a lack of insulin production or the body's cells not responding to insulin properly.

f) **Myopia or Short-Sightedness:** Myopia, a prevalent eye condition, results in distant objects appearing blurry while close objects remain clear.

26. Describe the pre-natal stages of development.

Ans. a) **Period of ovum:**

* Starts with conception to the end of the second week

*Practically size remains same because of the absence of external source of nourishment
*Rapid internal development
b) **Period of embryo**:
*End of second week to the end of second month
*All important external and internal features start to develop and function
*Sex organs develop well enough to distinguish the sex of the embryo
*By the end of the period, embryo measures 11⁄2 to 2 inches in length and weighs about 28.350 gms
*Growth in the head region is proportionately much greater than the rest of the body
*Accessory apparatus-placenta, umbilical cord and amniotic sac develops
c) **Period of foetus**:
* End of the second month to birth
* The baby's external and internal features are still growing and developing.
* By the fifth month, the internal organs are almost in their adult positions.
* Nerve cells are rapidly increasing in number during the second, third, and fourth months.
* Foetal activity starts in the second and third months of development.

****

Infancy and Early Childhood

1. A child in the age group of 0-2 years is known as an ---------------

Ans. Infant

2. Age from 3 to 6 years is known as --------------------

Ans. Early childhood

3. Early childhood is the preschool age and also known as ---------------------

Ans. Pre-gang age or age of exploration

4. -------------- skills are those which are performed using the large muscles of the body

Ans. Gross muscular skills

5. .... skills are those which involve the use of small muscles of the body.

Ans. Fine muscular skills

6. The production of meaningless speech sound consisting of two letter words is called ------------.

a) Babbling, b) Cooing, c) Crying, d) Gestures

Ans. a) Babbling

7. An explosive vowel like sound made by the child earlier around three months is called -----------.

Ans. Cooing

8. Identify the motor skill used by a child when he is buttoning his shirt, scribbling

and writing. (Sensory skill, Gross muscular skills, Fine muscular skills)

Ans. Fine muscular skills

9. First stage of cognitive development is called --------------- (sensory-motor stage)

10. --------- play is one in which the child makes something new by expressing his/her own ideas and feelings. (Manipulative play, Creative play, Physical play)

Ans. Creative play

11. During ---------------the hands, eyes and brain are being trained to co-ordinate, that is to work smoothly together.

a) Physical play, b) Social play, c) Manipulative play, d) Imaginative play

Ans. c) Manipulative play

12. Expand the following: a) ECCE b) ICDS

Ans. a) Early Childhood Care and Education

b) Integrated Child Development Services

13. Pick the odd one out:

a) Curiosity, b) Jealousy, c) Grief, d) Fear

Ans. a) Curiosity

14. Name any one manipulative play.

Ans. Sewing cards, threading beads.

15. The inability to take another person's perspective or point of view is called.........

a) Animism, b) Decentration, c) Centration, d) Egocentrism

Ans. Egocentrism

16. Attributing life to inanimate objects is called ----------------- (Animism)

17. Give an example of passive play.

Ans. Watching or listening to others, looking at pictures, listening to stories, watching Television, listening to music, etc.

18. Which type of nursery school utilised the benefits of ICDS?

Ans. Anganwadi

19. List the common emotions of early childhood.

Ans. Emotions can be broadly classified into two types:

a) Positive integrated emotions: Example Joy, love, affection, curiosity and sympathy.

b) Negative disintegrative emotions: Example Anger, fear, jealousy, grief.

20. -------------- provides a package of services namely, supplementary food, immunisation, health check up, referral services, non-formal preschool education and health and nutrition education for mothers.

Ans. Integrated Child Development Services (ICDS)

21. Find out the school that runs on the philosophy of Maria Montessori of Italy.

(Nursery School, Kindergarten, Montessori School)

Ans. Montessori School

22. Who developed the system of education known as 'Kindergarten' means 'Children's garden'.

Ans. Friedreich Froebel

23. ....helps the children to understand how people behave and also the world around them.

a)Manipulative play, b)Social play, c)Creative play, d)Imaginative play

Ans. Imaginative play

2 Mark Questions and Answers

24. Differentiate between Gross muscular skills and Fine muscular skills.

When it comes to physical activities, gross muscular skills refer to tasks that require the use of large muscle groups in the body, such as running, jumping, throwing and catching a ball, and climbing. In contrast, fine muscular skills involve using smaller muscles for activities like buttoning shirts, drawing, threading beads, writing, and scribbling.

25. Differentiate between creative play and imaginative play.

Ans. a) When children engage in creative play, they have the opportunity to express their ideas and emotions by making something new. They often use materials like blocks, sand, mud, clay, and beads to create various things.

b) Imaginative play involves children pretending to be someone else or even an animal. This type of play, also referred to as dramatic play or role play, helps children learn about human behavior and the world they live in. Children may pretend to be adults in roles such as doctors, teachers, or nurses.

3 Mark Questions and Answers

26. Explain any 3 characteristic features of cognitive development during early childhood.

Ans. According to Piaget, children in early childhood are in the Pre Operational stage of cognitive development, typically between ages 2 and 7. At this stage, they do not think logically but focus on learning language and symbolic thought. Three key features include:

1. Egocentrism: Children struggle to understand others' perspectives, such as believing the sun and moon are following them.

2. Animism: They attribute life-like qualities to non-living objects, like thinking stars twinkle because they are happy.

3. Irreversibility: Children find it difficult to mentally reverse a series of events.

27. Write a short note on socialization.

Ans. The growth of a child's social abilities happens through socialization. Socialization is the method of acquiring the abilities, outlooks, and actions that help individuals interact comfortably with family and society. It includes learning positive habits, ethics, religious and cultural principles, being disciplined, and developing a firm understanding of right and wrong. The child also learns essential social abilities such as teamwork, empathy, sharing, kindness, generosity, and more.

28. Elaborate the objectives of ECCE.

Ans. a) Setting the groundwork for a bright, fulfilling future by helping children reach their full potential.

b) Getting kids ready for starting and excelling in elementary school.

c) Offering assistance to women and girls to help them pursue education, training, and employment opportunities.

29. Summarise any three pre-speech forms of communication.

Ans. a) Crying: The baby expresses his needs only by crying during the first month. They cry to express hunger, pain, fatigue and to satisfy their desire for attention.

b) Cooing: Explosive vowel like sounds made by the child earlier around three months is called cooing. These early cooing sounds develop into babbling and later into words.

c) Babbling: Babbling is the production of inarticulate , meaningless speech sounds consisting of two letter words. eg. da-da, ma-ma. These gradually develop into words.

30. State the special features of Montessori approach in pre-school education.

Ans. These schools are based on the principles of Maria Montessori from Italy. The main focus of Montessori education is to understand the unique needs and abilities of each child.

1) Structured environment: The school offers a variety of special materials that allow children to develop cognitive skills in a carefully planned sequence. The teacher selects and organizes these materials, demonstrating how to use them. Children have the freedom to choose and work with the materials, leading to self-directed learning.

2) Individual activity: Emphasis is placed on individual activities and hands-on learning rather than group work. Each child is encouraged to learn at their own pace through independent activities. This allows for personalized learning experiences and encourages self-motivation.

c) Sensory learning: In Montessori education, students engage all their senses in learning. They interact with colors, numbers, shapes, and textures to fully immerse themselves in the learning experience.

31. Learning to speak involves three major tasks. Explain.

Ans. Learning to speak involves three major tasks. They are:

a) Pronunciation: When learning to speak, the first step is to pronounce words correctly. This skill is acquired through imitation.

b) Vocabulary building: Vocabulary development is the next phase, where children link meanings to the sounds of words. It is a more challenging task than pronunciation.

c) Sentence formation: As children progress, they learn to construct sentences by putting words together in a grammatically correct manner that can be easily comprehended by others. Initially, they may use simple one-word sentences, which, when accompanied by gestures, convey complete ideas.

32. Explain the characteristic features of sensory motor stage during infancy and early childhood.

Ans. During the first two years of life, children go through a stage where they do not use language and instead rely on their senses and motor skills to interact with their surroundings. They learn about the world by touching, tasting, and holding objects, developing an understanding of object permanence. This means they realize that objects continue to exist even when they are out of sight.

33. Write the objectives of Early Childhood Care and Education

* Building a strong foundation for a happy and successful life ahead by helping children reach their full potential.

* Getting kids ready for primary school and helping them succeed.

* Offering support to women and girls to access education, training, and employment opportunities.

34. Explain the features of ICDS

The program offers a variety of services including extra food, vaccinations, health exams, referrals, informal early childhood education, and health and nutrition education for mothers. The early childhood education focuses on the child and includes playful and recreational activities.

6 Mark Questions and Answers

35. Explain different categories of play.

Ans. Play may be divided into two categories. Active play and Passive play.

A) Active Play: When children engage in active play, they experience a sense of satisfaction from their actions. There are various forms of active play:

1) Exploratory play: This type of play allows children to investigate their surroundings and discover new things. For example, playing with a toy helps children understand its shape, texture, and color.

2) Physical play: This involves children participating in activities that involve movement, such as running, jumping, and climbing. It helps develop their gross motor skills.

3) Creative play: In creative play, children use their imagination to create something new by expressing their thoughts and emotions. For instance, children often build various things using blocks, sand, mud, clay, beads, etc.

4) Imaginative play: Children engage in imaginative play when they pretend to be someone else and act out different roles.

d) Imaginative play: It helps them to understand how people behave and also the world around them. The child acts out adult roles like doctor, teacher, nurse, etc.

e) Manipulative play is all about using your hands skillfully. It helps train your hands, eyes, and brain to work together. Activities like sewing cards, threading beads, and drawing are great for manipulative play.

f) Social play is when children play together. It helps them learn how to cooperate, share, and be honest with each other.

B) Passive play is when children take a more passive role in activities. They enjoy watching or listening to others. Examples of passive play include watching others, looking at pictures, listening to stories, and watching television.

36. **Describe the importance/need of ECCE in the life of an individual.**

Ans. a) The growth and development in childhood, encompassing physical, cognitive, and social-emotional domains, progress swiftly. The home setting may not fully address these needs, underscoring the importance of early childhood educational facilities.

b) Early childhood experiences, characterized by richness and challenges, have the capacity to shape an individual's habits, attitudes, trust in others, and more.

c) Play is a fundamental avenue for learning in children. Early childhood care and education offer opportunities for social interaction and skill development through group play experiences, facilitating effective social integration.

d) It has been shown that children who have participated in early childhood education programs excel and adapt easily in primary school. They are also equipped with the necessary concepts for formal learning.

e) These programs offer a conducive environment for children, including those from cramped urban apartments with limited space and those from slum areas and impoverished households with inadequate home conditions.

f) Additionally, the program ensures that the nutritional and healthcare needs of children from economically disadvantaged backgrounds are met.

37. **Write the importance of play or the significance of play in the life of young children.**

Ans. Playing is important for children as it helps them learn about themselves and the world around them. It gives them the opportunity to explore, experiment, create, focus, communicate thoughts, build physical strength, innovate, acquire new abilities, work together, unleash their creativity, pretend, improve communication skills, collaborate, and show concern for others.

a) Playing leads to happiness: When a child is engaged in play, they are more likely to feel happy because play can create a sense of satisfaction and accomplishment.

b) Playing helps prevent boredom: It is crucial to keep children from getting bored, as boredom can quickly lead to moodiness, irritability, and destructive behavior.

c) Playing reduces stress: Acting out stressful scenarios during play can help children prepare for and cope with real-life stressors.

d) Playing redirects aggressive instincts: By allowing children to release negative emotions through play, they can learn to manage their aggression in a socially acceptable way.

38. Describe positive integrative emotions of a child.

Ans. Positive integrative emotions are nice to have. They make a person feel happy and are well-received by others. Examples include joy, love, affection, curiosity, and sympathy.

a) Curiosity: Children often ask questions such as 'what is this?' when they are young. Curiosity is the fascination with new, unfamiliar or mysterious things in a person's surroundings. It is the longing to learn.

b) Joy, pleasure, and delight: Joy is a positive feeling. It is referred to as pleasure, delight, or happiness. Children show their joy through smiling, laughing, clapping their hands, and showing affection through hugs and kisses.

c) Affection: Affection is an emotional response aimed towards a person, an animal, or an object. It demonstrates warm feelings, friendliness, sympathy, or helpfulness and can be shown through physical actions or words.

39. Play promotes the all round development of young children. Justify the statement.

Ans. "Play is incredibly important for young children's development. It helps them grow physically, emotionally, mentally, socially, and morally. The benefits of play for children include:"

a) Physical value: Play is important for the physical development of children as it provides exercise for their bodies, helps in developing motor coordination, and promotes good sleep and appetite.

b) Social value: Play is a valuable socializing force for children as they learn important skills such as giving and taking in the playground. It also helps in expanding the child's social contacts, teaching them how to play fair, work as part of a team, be loyal to others, and handle criticism.

c) Educational value: Play has educational benefits as well, helping children improve their intellectual skills by learning different concepts such as shape, size, number, and texture through play. Activities like exploring and collecting play objects help children gather information about their environment and stimulate their imagination.

40. Explain the motor development during infancy and early childhood period

Through motor development, children naturally acquire a variety of motor skills, which can be separated into two categories: gross muscular skills and fine muscular skills.

Gross muscular skills involve actions that utilize the larger muscle groups in the body, such as running, jumping, throwing and catching a ball, and climbing. On the other hand, fine muscular skills refer to tasks that require the use of smaller muscle groups, like buttoning shirts, drawing, threading beads, writing, and scribbling.

Both gross and fine muscular skills are essential for the coordination and movement of hands and legs. During infancy, the focus of hand skills typically revolves around fostering independence in activities like feeding, dressing, and playing. Similarly, leg skills are crucial during infancy as they are vital for the development of walking abilities.

****

CHAPTER IV

Late Childhood Years

1.The period of late childhood is often referred as ----------------- (school years)

2. ------------- mean any form of appreciation for an attainment. (Rewards)

3. A deviation in behaviour from the one expected or approved by the group is called ----------

Ans. Behaviour problem

4. Identify the characteristics of social development in which children choose friends of their own sex and show hostility towards the members of the opposite sex.

Ans. Sex antagonism

5. Identify the odd one : Competition, suggestibility, consistency, responsibility.

Ans. Consistency

6. The disciplinary method with strict rules and regulations, no freedom of action, movement and thoughts and too much emphasis on perfection. Suggest the name of this disciplinary approach.

Ans. Authoritarian disciplinary technique.

7. Disciplinary techniques which allows self discipline and self control is --------------

Ans. Democratic disciplinary technique.

8. The school years are usually referred to as ---------age.

Ans. gang age.

9. During stage the child enters the period of concrete operations in thinking.

Ans. the late childhood

10. The skills which help the child to become sociable at home and school.

a)Play skills, b)School skills, c)Social help skills, d)Self help skills

Ans. c)Social help skills

11. Choose the right example for social help skills from the following:

a)Emptying dust bin, b)Bath and groom with speed, c) Clay modeling, d) Writing

Ans. a) Emptying dust bin

12. Discipline has four essential elements. Explain any two.

Ans. Discipline includes four key components: Rules, Consistency, Punishment, and Rewards.

a) Rules: The foundation of discipline lies in having clear rules. Rules outline the expected behavior and boundaries for children. They offer guidelines for appropriate actions in various situations and aid in the development of moral values.

b) Consistency: Consistent enforcement of rules is crucial for effective discipline. Maintaining consistency helps children learn and adapt faster to the expected behaviors.

13. **Write a short note on social help skills.**

Ans. Social skills are important for children to develop in order to become more sociable both at home and at school. This can involve helping out with chores such as dusting and assisting in the kitchen at home. Similarly, at school children can develop these skills by tasks like cleaning the blackboard or emptying the waste paper basket.

14. **Suggest some measures to overcome behavior problems among children.**

Ans. a) Show love to the child so he can build confidence in himself and others.

b) Acknowledge his value as an individual.

c) Honor his rights and guide him to comprehend and honor the rights of others.

d) Support him in cultivating initiative, imagination, and creativity.

15. **What is your opinion about democratic disciplinary technique?**

Ans. The best disciplinary technique is the democratic approach. This method involves using explanations, discussions, and reasoning to help children understand the reasons behind expected behavior. It focuses on fostering growth, self-discipline, and self-control without resorting to harsh punishments. Positive reinforcement, such as praise, is given when children meet or exceed expectations.

3 Mark questions and answers

16. **What are the causes of behavioural problems among children?**

Ans. a) Children may struggle when they are in an environment that does not allow them to freely express themselves.

b) Children can feel overwhelmed when parents and teachers have high expectations that they cannot meet.

c) Children may resort to negative behaviors as a way to get what they desire.

d) Family issues can impact a child's well-being.

e) Crisis situations in a child's life can have a significant impact on their emotional and mental health.

17. **Describe the principles governing habit formation.**

Ans. The principles governing habit formation are:

a) **The principle of repetition** states that for an action to become a habit, it must be done multiple times.

b) **The principle of effect** emphasizes that the initial impact of an action on a child will determine if they continue to do it.

c) **The principle of learning and unlearning** highlights that habits can be both learned and unlearned. If an action is not repeated, it may eventually fade away.

d) **The principle of continuity and consistency** underscores the importance of consistently repeating an action for it to become a habit. Parents play a crucial role in enforcing and encouraging good habits in their children. Providing explanations about the benefits of good habits and the drawbacks of bad habits can aid in habit formation.

18. Late childhood is a period of learning motor skills. Explain any three motor skills of late childhood.

Ans. 1) **Self help skills** – These are essential for individuals to take care of themselves, such as eating, dressing, and bathing.

2) **School skills** – They are necessary for students to excel in their academic pursuits, including writing, drawing, painting, and singing.

3) **Play skills** – These are important for children to participate in recreational activities, such as throwing and catching balls, riding bicycles, and skipping.

19. Some parents consider discipline as harmful because it limits a child's freedom to develop in his or her own way. Do you agree with this statement? Give reasons.

Harmful Effects of Too Much Discipline:

- Too much discipline is not good.
- Strict rules and no freedom can be harmful.

Authoritarian Discipline Drawbacks:

- Authoritarian technique focuses too much on perfection.
- Strict rules and no freedom are not beneficial.

Benefits of Democratic Discipline:

- Democratic methods explain, discuss, and reason.
- Help children grow, develop self-discipline, and self-control.

Positive Outcomes for Children in Democratic Way:

- Children raised democratically become independent thinkers.
- They develop a healthy, positive, and confident self-concept.
- Achieve greater creativity.

20. Importance of Good Discipline:

- Good discipline makes a child feel secure.
- Teaches what is safe and unsafe.
- Helps develop self-control.

- Shapes and perfects behavior.

21. In your opinion, which disciplinary technique is most effective? Why?

Ans. Using a democratic approach to discipline is proven to be the most successful way to help children learn and grow. This method focuses on explaining, discussing, and reasoning with the child to help them understand the reasons behind expected behavior. It prioritizes personal development, self-discipline, and self-control without resorting to harsh punishments. Instead, positive reinforcement through praise is used to recognize and encourage children when they meet expectations.

22. Explain the significant characteristics of social development during late childhood years.

Ans. a)Formation of childhood gangs: When children form gangs, it's usually because they share common interests and enjoy spending time together. Being part of a gang can help a child learn how to behave socially.

b) Oversensitivity: Children often feel very sensitive and can get upset quickly if they are scolded or feel threatened.

c) Suggestibility: Kids are quite suggestible, meaning they are easily swayed by the opinions and actions of those around them, especially their friends.

23. Explain the characteristics of cognitive development during late childhood years.

Growing Perceptual Powers:As children grow older, their perception becomes more accurate and detailed. They also develop a longer memory during this time. In terms of cognitive skills, they enter the stage of concrete operations in their thinking. During this stage, children exhibit , decentration by being able to shift their attention from one aspect to another, showing a flexible problem-solving approach. For example, they can group cows as both animals and animals that give milk. They also demonstrate reversibility by understanding that processes can go both ways. For instance, they recognize that subtraction is the reverse of addition, understanding cause-effect relationships. Another important cognitive skill that develops during this time is conservation. Children learn that something can remain the same despite changes in appearance. For instance, they understand the conservation of numbers by realizing that the quantity of numbers remains constant even if they are rearranged.

24. Analyse the major tasks in learning to speak in late childhood years.

- **Vocabulary:** During this stage of development, children expand their vocabulary by learning new words and understanding different meanings for words they already know. Typically, girls tend to acquire a larger vocabulary compared to boys.
- **Pronunciation:** Additionally, errors in pronunciation become less frequent as children get older. Pronunciation can be influenced by a child's geographical location and family upbringing.
- **Sentence Construction:** By the age of six, children are capable of constructing various types of sentences. The complexity and length of sentences continue to increase until around nine or ten years old.

25. Evaluate the different techniques of discipline.

Ans. The different disciplinary techniques are:

a) Authoritarian disciplinary technique: The authoritarian disciplinary technique involves strict rules and regulations, limited freedom, and a focus on perfection. Children face constant criticism, have no respect for their individual rights, and are controlled through punishment. They are not involved in decision-making and receive no recognition for meeting expectations.

b) Permissive disciplinary technique: A permissive disciplinary approach involves minimal to no use of discipline. It lacks guidance for children and avoids punishment. Boundaries are not clearly established for the child, allowing them to make their own decisions with excessive leniency.

c) Democratic disciplinary techniques: Democratic disciplinary methods employ explanations, discussion and reasoning to help the child understand why they are expected to behave in a certain way. They emphasize growth, self-discipline and self-control. There is no harsh punishment at any time. Reward with praise is given when the child comes up to expected standards.

****

CHAPTER V

Adolescence – Charms and Challenges

1 Mark questions and answers

1. Adolescence period is also known as ------------------------

Ans. Teen age or period of storm and stress

2. The sudden increase in height and weight of an individual that turns children into adolescents.

Ans. Growth spurt

3. ----------- is a group of individuals of the same age, social status, ability, who are considered to share similar values and interests.

Ans. Peer group

4. --------------is an eating disorder characterised by Binge-Purge eating pattern.

Ans. Bulimia Nervosa

5. ------------------ is a complex eating disorder characterised by self starvation and severe loss of weight which can lead to death

Ans. Anorexia Nervosa

6. Expand the term BMI

Ans. Body Mass Index

7. The formula for calculating BMI is-----------------

Ans. Weight in kilogram divided by the square of height in meters.

8. The process of forming identity is called--------------------------

Ans. Identity formation.

9. ----------------- is the development of the distinct personality of an individual.

Ans. Identity formation

10. Individual's perception of one's qualities, competencies are called -------.

Ans. Self concept

11. One's thoughts and feelings about oneself

Ans. Self esteem

12. The categorisation of overweight or obesity is done based on --------------

Ans. Body Mass Index (BMI).

13. -------------- is choosing to do something under the influence of peers.

Ans. Peer pressure

14. List the consequences of Anorexia Nervosa.

Ans. a) Change in heart beat

b) Dehydration, kidney problems

c) Liver damage

d) Amenorrhea-menstruation stops

15. Which of the following statement shows the ability of propositional thinking?

a) He will reason out imaginary situations.

b) He can imagine the objects based on verbal statements.

c) He is capable of imagining all the alternatives for solving a given problem.

Ans. b) He can imagine the objects based on verbal statements.

16. Name any one adolescent eating disorder.

Ans. Anorexia Nervosa

17. If a person is overweight, his BMI is between.......................

Ans. 25 to 29.910. Calculate the BMI of an adolescent boy having 60 kg weight and 1.60 metres of height. Identify to which category of BMI he belongs.

a) Under weight, b) Normal weight, c) Over weight, d) Obese

Ans. BMI can be calculated by weight in kilograms divided by the square of height in metres. Therefore 60 divided by 1.6 x 1.6 = 23.4. Category of weight is Normal Weight.

18. If your BMI is 26.7 in which category of weight do you belong to?

Ans. Over weight

19. If your BMI is above 30, which category of weight do you belong?

Ans. Obese

20. The formula used to calculate the BMI is.......................

Ans. Weight in kg divided by height in metre square.

21. Name an adolescent eating disorder characterised by self-starvation and severe loss of weight which can lead to death.

Ans. Anorexia Nervosa

3 Mark Questions and answers

22. Describe identity formation. There are 3 general aspects for identity formation. Evaluate.

Ans. Identity is the way we see ourselves through our roles in society, known as identity formation. This process shapes our unique personality. There are three key aspects to identity formation:

a) Self-concept: One's self concept is an individual's perception of one's own qualities, competencies, etc. This is how we view our own qualities and abilities.

b) Sense of identity: This is our understanding of who we are as individuals, influenced by our environment.

c) Self esteem: This is our self-perception and feelings about ourselves. It is essential for cultivating a positive outlook on life.

23. Explain the causes and consequences of substance abuse.

Causes of Substance Abuse:

- Curiosity: Adolescents may try drugs out of curiosity, leading to chronic use and abuse.
- Parental Modelling and Peer Pressure: Teens are more likely to use substances if their parents and peers do.
- Rebellion against Norms: Some adolescents use substances to defy parents, teachers, or societal norms.

Consequences of Substance Abuse:

- Academics: Substance abuse is linked to low grades, school absences, and dropouts.
- Physical Health: Serious health issues like cardiovascular diseases, cancer, HIV/AIDS, and more can result. Substance use increases the risk of death through various means.
- Mental Health: Substance abuse can lead to mental health problems such as depression, suicidal thoughts etc.

24. Specify the characteristics of early maturing boys during adolescence.

Ans. Boys who mature early are typically taller and stronger than their peers. They tend to be more popular and are frequently chosen for sports and other activities. They also have a positive body image, with higher levels of confidence, security, and independence. These boys may exhibit more aggressiveness and are more likely to engage in risky behaviors, often losing interest in academic studies.

25. Write short notes on the consequences of adolescent pregnancy.

Ans. Adolescent pregnancies pose health risks for both the baby and the mother. Infants born to adolescent mothers are at higher risk of low birth weight, neurological issues, and childhood illnesses, which can ultimately lead to infant mortality. Pregnant adolescents are also more susceptible to unsafe abortions compared to adults, leading to potential complications like anemia and prolonged labor. Furthermore, these young mothers may experience long-term health issues, drop out of school, and face poverty.

26. Write short notes on identity crisis during adolescents.

Ans. Identity crisis is a state or period of psychological distress occurring in adolescence when they have difficulty in understanding the changes their bodies are going through, or, have not achieved the sense of self identity. It is a period of uncertainty and confusion due to a change in their expected aims or role in society.

27. How can you manage bulimia nervosa?

Ans. Counseling therapy is beneficial for individuals struggling with bulimia. It is important for them to acknowledge that they are dealing with a problem. Medications can aid in disrupting addictive behaviors, and antidepressants may be prescribed as well.

28. Suggest methods to solve emotional problems among adolescents.

Ans. a) Build a strong sense of self-worth and belief in yourself.

b) Focus on your own journey instead of comparing yourself to others.

c) Share your feelings and concerns with trusted family members or friends to find solutions to emotional challenges.

d) Steer clear of triggering situations that may lead to emotional outbursts.

29. Compare the advantages of early and late maturation in boys.

Ans. a)Early maturation in boys: During early maturation, boys experience benefits such as increased height and strength compared to their peers, making them more popular and likely to be chosen for sports and other activities. They also tend to have a positive body image, increased confidence, and independence.

b)Late maturation in boys: On the other hand, late maturing boys often display greater intellectual curiosity, social initiative, and creative problem-solving skills as they transition into adulthood.

30. Differentiate between Anorexia Nervosa and Bulimia Nervosa.

Ans. a) Anorexia Nervosa is a serious eating disorder where individuals starve themselves and experience extreme weight loss, which can be fatal. Those affected by this disorder often fear gaining weight and may skip meals, leading to a distorted body image.

b) Bulimia Nervosa is another eating disorder marked by a binge-purge eating cycle. People with bulimia consume large amounts of high-calorie foods and then purge through self-induced vomiting or the use of laxatives.

4 Mark questions and answers

31. How does relationship with peers affect the social development of children during adolescence?

Definition: A peer group is a bunch of people the same age, social status, and ability, who share similar values and interests.

Influence of Peer Groups:

- Behavior and Attitude: Adolescents' actions and attitudes are significantly shaped by their peer group.
- Development of Skills: Peer groups help develop physical and social skills.
- Social Skills: Learning empathy, sharing, and leadership through peer interactions.
- Positive Influences: Peers can positively influence academics, motivation, clothing style, language, and vocabulary.
- Security and Support: Peer groups provide a sense of security and moral support.
- Role in Psycho-Social Development: Peer groups play a crucial role in forming the identity of adolescents.

32. Suggest some effective strategies to manage adolescent stress.

Ans. a) Think positively and optimistically: A positive mood improves self esteem and an optimistic attitude improves self efficiency and increases self control. With better self control, stressful situations can be avoided.

b) Seek social support: Support from family members, friends, teachers, etc. can help to reduce stress. The adolescent can also seek professional help from counsellors or therapists.

33. Adolescence has certain characteristics that distinguish it from other periods. Justify.
a) A Significant Period:

- Adolescence is crucial because individuals start thinking seriously about themselves.
- This phase brings physical, biological, and psychological changes, forming new attitudes, values, and interests.

b) Transitional Phase:

- Adolescence is a transition from childhood to adulthood.
- Neither a child nor an adult, individuals have left childhood behind but haven't reached full adult maturity.

c) Problem Age:

- Adolescents face tensions, worries, and anxieties due to clashes with parents, increased peer interactions, heightened emotions, and hormonal changes.

d) Time of Identity Formation:

- Adolescence is when individuals develop a distinct personality.
- Crucial choices are made, shaping roles and values that determine identity.

e) Unrealistic Aspirations:

- Adolescents often have unrealistic expectations for themselves and others.
- Society imposes many expectations, leading to potential disappointments.

f) Threshold of Adulthood:

- Adolescents may experiment with socially unacceptable adult behaviors like smoking and drinking to create the impression of being adults.

6 Mark questions and answers

34. Evaluate the causes, consequences and management of adolescent obesity.
Causes of Adolescent Obesity:

- **Hereditary Factors:** Some teens inherit the tendency to be overweight, often from obese parents.
- **Environmental Factors:**

  - **Dietary Patterns:** Unhealthy eating habits like fast food, soft drinks, and high-calorie non-vegetarian foods contribute to obesity.
  - **Decrease in Physical Activity:** Obese teens are less active. Those involved in sports and exercise are less likely to be overweight.

B. Consequences of Adolescent Obesity:

- **Biological Development Effects:** Obesity in teens can lead to health issues like high blood pressure, hip problems, pulmonary issues, heart diseases, and diabetes.
- **Socio-Emotional Development Effects:** Obese teens often have lower self-esteem, a less positive self-image, are prone to depression, and face more peer relationship problems.

C. Managing Adolescent Obesity:

- **Calorie Intake Restriction:** Encouraging healthier eating habits and discouraging unhealthy foods can be effective.
- **Regular Exercise:** Promoting exercise programs, including activities like walking, cycling, and swimming, helps combat obesity.

35. Evaluate the causes of adolescent stress and suggest some effective strategies to manage such disorder.
A. Causes of Adolescent Stress:
a) Physical Factors:

- Adolescents go through physical changes, leading to mood swings, low self-esteem, anxiety, and depression.
- Coping with body changes and mood fluctuations can cause stress.

b) Social Factors:

- Social pressure, trying to gain friends' approval, and peer pressure for risky behaviors (smoking, drugs) cause stress.
- Engaging in early sexual behavior due to peer influence can also lead to stress.

c) Academic Factors:

- Academic pressure, like getting good grades and completing assignments, is a major cause of stress.
- High expectations from parents and teachers contribute to stress.

B. Managing Adolescent Stress:
a) Think Positively:

- Positive thinking improves self-esteem, and an optimistic attitude increases self-control.

- Avoiding stress by choosing productive activities instead of distracting ones like smoking and drinking.

b) Seek Social Support:

- Support from family, friends, and teachers helps reduce stress.
- Professional help from counselors or therapists is an option.

c) Use Multiple Coping Strategies:

- Choosing more than one strategy is effective in managing stress.

36. Explain the causes and consequences of anorexia Nervosa.
A. Causes of Anorexia Nervosa:

- **Psychological Factors:** Anorexia is linked to perfectionism, overachievement, low self-esteem, emotional disturbances, and traumatic experiences.
- **Social and Family Factors:** Cultural influences, peer pressure, and family dynamics can contribute to anorexia.
- **Biological Factors:** Genetic predisposition, brain chemistry (high cortisol, low serotonin), and stressful events play a role.

B. Consequences of Anorexia Nervosa:

- Change in Heartbeat
- Dehydration, Kidney Problems
- Liver Damage

- Amenorrhea (Menstruation Stops)
- Wastage of Muscles (Weakness and Loss of Function)
- Slowed Digestion, Constipation, and Abdominal Pain

37. Explain management of substance abuse among adolescents.

Ans. Drug rehabilitation is a form of medical and psychological treatment that helps individuals overcome substance abuse and reintegrate into society as productive members. Medication can be used to control physical dependence on addictive substances, while therapy in a supportive environment and increased parental involvement can help address psychological dependency. Engaging in social activities also plays a role in helping individuals adjust to life without drugs.

38. Suggest some management techniques for adolescents having anorexia nervosa.

Ans. a) Medical treatment: To begin with, the most important aspect of medical care is addressing critical health issues to ensure stability. In severe cases, hospitalization may be necessary until a healthy weight is attained.

b) Nutritional treatment: nutritional counseling plays a key role in the treatment process. A nutritionist can assist in creating meal plans that supply sufficient calories and protein to sustain a normal body weight.

c) Counselling therapy: counseling therapy focuses on recognizing and changing negative thoughts and emotions that contribute to the disorder. It also helps individuals manage challenging feelings, relationship issues, and stress in a constructive manner. Family therapy can also be beneficial in this process.

39. Evaluate the causes and consequences of Bulimia Nervosa.

Ans. A. Causes of Bulimia Nervosa:

a) Body image obsession: Body image obsession is a common issue among many adolescents who may turn to a bulimic lifestyle in order to achieve a slim physique. The pressure from peers and societal standards can contribute to this behavior.

b) Low self esteem: Individuals struggling with bulimia often have low self-esteem and view weight loss as a means to gain self-worth.

c) Depression: People with bulimia are depressed and they overeat and try to get rid of it. Depression is frequently seen in individuals with bulimia, leading to overeating and subsequent attempts to purge.

d) Stress: Stressful life events, such as the loss of a loved one or family conflict, can trigger bulimic behavior in some individuals.

B. Consequences of Bulimia Nervosa:

- Self induced vomiting can lead to irritations and bleeding in the lining of throat, oesophagus and stomach.
- Loss of muscle mass and body weight
- Excessive vomiting and laxative use can lead to electrolyte imbalances due to sodium and potassium loss
- Stomach acid from vomiting can damage tooth enamel.

40. Elucidate the social development during adolescence.

a) Relationship with Parents:

- Adolescents often clash with parents during puberty, leading to conflicts over control.
- Arguments arise as adolescents resist parental interference in their behavior and values.
- Criticism and questioning of authority increase during this phase.
- Teens who have a good relationship with parents are less likely to engage in risky behaviors.

b) Relationship with Peers:

- Peers have a big influence on adolescents' social development.
- Peer groups, consisting of individuals of the same age and interests, shape behaviors and attitudes.
- Positive peer influence includes academic motivation, clothing style, and language.
- Peer groups offer a sense of security and moral support, aiding in identity formation.
- Negative peer influence can lead to experimentation with drugs, drinking, and smoking.

c) Relationship with Teachers:

- Schools play a major role in teaching social and academic skills to adolescents.
- The school environment and teachers influence the personality of adolescents.
- Teachers should be excellent role models and friends, recognizing hidden talents in students.

41. Elaborate any three characteristics of adolescent cognitive development.
a) Hypothetic-Deductive Reasoning:

- **Definition:** Adolescents can imagine various solutions to a problem, shifting from real to possible thoughts.
- **Example:** When asked about a woman's death with a heated iron nearby, a younger child might assume electric shock. The adolescent considers all possibilities before concluding.

b) Propositional Thinking:

- **Definition:** Adolescents can reason out verbal propositions without needing to see the objects.
- **Example:** An adolescent can compare the height of three dolls based on verbal descriptions without seeing them.

c) Systematic Thinking:

- **Definition:** Adolescents can think systematically to solve problems.
- **Example:** Given letters A, T, E, and M to form words, an adolescent systematically creates all possible words. A child without a systematic approach will generate fewer words.

42. Analyse the causes and consequences of adolescent depression.

Ans. A. Causes of adolescent depression:

a) Genetic factors: Genetic factors play a role in the development of depression, as studies have shown that individuals with a family history of the disorder are more likely to experience it themselves.

b)Biological factors: Biological factors can also contribute to depression, such as imbalances in neurotransmitters like serotonin. In women, fluctuations in reproductive hormones like estrogen and progesterone can also be linked to mood disorders.

c)Family and social factors: Family dynamics and social interactions can also play a significant role in the onset of depression. Factors such as conflicts between parents and adolescents, lack of parental support, and marital discord can all contribute to depressive symptoms in young people. Social factors like not having a close friend, facing rejection from peers, and having difficulties in romantic relationships can further exacerbate feelings of sadness and loneliness.

B. Consequences of Depression:

a) Having trouble focusing, struggling with school work, and facing challenges in relationships with parents and peers.

b) Finding it hard to participate in daily activities and fulfill responsibilities.

c) Experiencing health issues like stomach pain, tiredness, and headaches.

43. Discuss the causes and management of adolescent pregnancy.

Ans. A. Causes of adolescent pregnancy:

a) One common issue in many cultures is early marriage, where girls are often forced into marriage at a young age and expected to start having children.

b) Education plays a significant role in preventing early pregnancies, as women with higher levels of education tend to have lower birth rates. Lack of comprehensive sex education also contributes to the issue.

c) Another contributing factor is sexual abuse, particularly among adolescent girls. This can occur within families or outside of them, putting young girls at risk of exploitation and harm.

B. Managing adolescent pregnancy: Teenage mothers require substantial support to improve their chances in education and employment. It is crucial to provide them with the necessary resources to excel in childcare and to make plans for their future. Offering appropriate family and sex education can help lower the incidence of teenage pregnancy.

****

CHAPTER VI

Adulthood and Old Age

1 mark questions and answers

1. The adulthood period is also known as the period of -----------------

Ans. Responsibility

2. -------------------- is the stage of human development having longest age span

Ans. Adulthood

6 Mark questions and answers

3. **Describe the responsibilities of adulthood**

Adults have responsibilities in three main areas, namely Choosing a career, Choosing a life partner and Maintaining family.

A. Choosing a career

In order to make future responsibilities fruitful an adult needs a good career. Career is a job which helps one to earn for his/her living.

a. Responsibility towards authority: When it comes to authority, career-oriented individuals should be prepared to work to their full potential, continuously improve their skills, and be willing to make personal sacrifices for both their own well-being and the well-being of the organization.

b. Towards co-workers, subordinates and workplace: In terms of interactions with co-workers and subordinates, collaboration is key for a more efficient work environment. It not only enhances job satisfaction but also eliminates professional jealousy and rivalry. Authorities should maintain a friendly atmosphere with their subordinates to ensure their comfort.

c. Towards specific work: Each job requires specific talents and skills for effective performance. It is important to understand the unique demands of a job in order to excel in it.

B. Choosing a Life Partner

The responsibilities included in marriage are responsibility towards the mate and responsibility towards in-laws.

a. Towards the mate: a. In a marriage, both partners must be willing to compromise and make sacrifices in order to accommodate each other. It is important for husband and wife to care for each other, show mutual love, share interests, and offer support.

b. Towards in- laws: When it comes to relationships with in-laws, newlywed couples may find it challenging to accept advice, guidance, and financial assistance. However, it is crucial for young adults to show respect, care, and love towards their in-laws and other family members. Additionally, the younger generation should provide financial support to their elderly parents and in-laws.

C. Maintaining a Family

The pattern of family life undergoes marked changes during the period of middle age. For the smooth running of the family all the members should take up certain responsibilities.

a. Responsibility as a good parent: a. When it comes to being a good parent, it is essential for parents to provide care and show concern for their children. Children require a solid education, a strong moral compass, good physical health, and more. It is the duty of parents to fulfill these needs.

b. Responsibility towards other family members: Adults also have a responsibility towards other members of the family. This includes offering care, respect, and protection to elderly parents and in-laws. Grandparents should be given the opportunity to take on certain responsibilities in raising the children.

c. Responsibility towards the living society: It is important for adults to fulfill their responsibilities towards the broader society. This includes responsibilities towards the neighborhood, relatives, and the community as a whole. Being productive and taking responsibility for the betterment of society should never be overlooked.

4. List out the characteristics of old age

Ans. The characteristics of old age are:

- Decreased overall attractiveness and loss of productivity
- Financial concerns and feelings of poor health
- Decline in cognitive abilities leading to slower thinking and learning, forgetfulness, confusion, repetitive speech, and quick fatigue
- Sense of worthlessness, insecurity, loneliness, and self-centeredness
- Appearance changes such as wrinkles, liver spots, and gray or white hair
- Decline in sense organs, immune system, circulatory system, blood flow, and lung capacity
- Changes in vocal cords resulting in an elderly-sounding voice
- Decreased eyesight and difficulty reading in low light conditions.

5. Explain the physical needs of oldage

Ans. The oldage need physical help in the following matters:

- **Constant Support :** Old people need help because their senses, energy, and body functions decline. They require ongoing assistance.
- **Changes in Living : Ageing** demands adjustments in homes and surroundings. This includes changes inside and outside, good lighting, and helpful devices like walking sticks.
- **Healthcare Needs:** Chronic illnesses and diseases need regular checkups and medicines. Visiting doctors and mobile clinics are very helpful.

- **Healthy Eating:** Older people need good, healthy, and easy-to-digest food to manage weakness and digestion problems.
- **Travel Companionship:** They often need a friend to help when traveling.

6. List out the main reasons for Choosing a Home Outside

- **Family Conflicts:** Conflicts with family members can make people choose a home outside.
- **Loneliness :** Feeling lonely and sad, no matter education or income, is a big reason.
- **Lost Touch with Family:** Losing touch with family due to children's marriage or job demands can lead to this choice.
- **Lack of Social Connections:** Not having family or friends around is another reason.
- **Death of Life Partner :** The death of a spouse can bring great sadness and make someone choose to live elsewhere.
- **Difficulty with Environment:** Struggling to adjust to changes in the surroundings is a common reason.
- **Health and Self-Care:** Being sick and unable to care for oneself is a factor.
- **Lack of Support:** Not having someone to provide care and support influences the decision.

7. Explain the merits and demerits of old age homes or choosing home outside during oldage
Merits:

- **Maintenance and Repair Services**: Old age homes provide maintenance and repair services for residents.
- **Affordable Meals:** Residents get all meals at reasonable costs.
- **Recreational Opportunities:** The homes offer suitable recreations and amusements
- **Social Connections:** Opportunities to connect with peers who share similar interests and abilities.
- **Companionship:** Eliminates loneliness as people are always available for companionship.
- **Holiday Celebrations:** Special celebrations for those without family during holidays.
- **Prestige Opportunities:** Opportunities for prestige based on past accomplishments.

Demerits:

- **Higher Expenses:** Living in old age homes is more expensive than in one's own home.
- **Unappealing Institutional Food:** Food provided by the institution is usually less appealing than homemade food.
- **Limited Food Choices:** The choice of food is limited, and there's a lack of variety.
- **Uncongenial Company:** Close and constant contact with people who may be unpleasant.
- **Isolation from Amenities:** Locations are usually away from shops, amusements, and community organizations.
- **Separation from Family and Friends:** Living in old age homes is away from family and friends.

- **Smaller Living Quarters:** Living quarters tend to be considerably smaller than one's home.
- **Limited Opportunities with Younger People :** Opportunities for acceptance by contemporaries are greater than with younger people.

****

CHAPTER VII

Childhood Diseases and Prevention

1 Mark questions and answers

1. A pre-milk substance containing antibodies and white cells from the mother's blood is called ---------------

Ans. Colustrum

2. Breast feeding provides ----------------- immunity

Ans. naturally acquired passive immunity

3. Expand the terms.

(a) **DTP** – Diphtheria, Tetanus, Pertusis (b) **OPV** – Oral Polio Vaccine

(c) **CRS** - Congenital Rubella Syndrome (d) **BCG** - Bacille Calmette-Guerin

(d) **DOTS** - Directly Observed Treatment, Short-course

(e) **MMR** – Mumps, Measles, Rubella (f) **TB** - Tuberculosis

4. Diseases and causing Organisms

Diphtheria - Coryne Bacterium Diphtheria *(Bacteria)*

Tetanus - Clostridium tetani *(Bacteria)*

Polio - Polio Virus

Tuberculosis - Mycobacterium Tuberculosis *(Bacteria)*

5. Vaccination provides .... immunity

Ans. Artificially acquired active immunity

6. Breast milk is an example for .... immunity

Ans. Naturally Acquired passive immunity

7. .... is caused by a virus that affects liver.

Ans. Hepatitis B

8. .... is a crippling disease caused by a virus

Ans. Poliomyelitis

9. .... vaccine is given for preventing TB

Ans. BCG

10. Odd one outbursts

a) Syphilis b) AIDS c) Tetanus d) Gonorrhoea

Ans. Tetanus

11. **Define immunity.**

Immunity is the specific resistance to a disease and involves the production of an antibody against a specific antigen.

12. **Explain the different types of Immunity (Defence Mechanisms)**

A. Non-Specific Immunity (Non-Specific Defence Mechanisms)

The immune system works to protect the body from various foreign threats. Examples of non-specific defense mechanisms include the skin, tears, neutrophils, monocytes, stomach acid, vomiting, bowel movements, and urination.

B. Specific Immunity (Specific Defence Mechanisms)

These are the last line of defence against illness. Special mechanisms can identify and react to particular substances.

Types of Specific Immunity (Specific Defence Mechanisms)

Specific immunity can also be classified into two main categories: inborn and acquired

a. Inborn immunity (inherited or innate immunity): Inborn immunity refers to the immunity that is inherited or genetic.

b. Acquired immunity: Acquired immunity is attained through natural or artificial means.

1. **Naturally acquired immunity**: Natural immunity happens when someone comes into contact with a germ. This can happen through either active exposure or passive transfer.

i. Naturally acquired active immunity: When a child is exposed to and contracts a disease, their immune system naturally develops immunity. eg.***Measles or chickenpox***

ii. Naturally acquired passive immunity: Naturally acquired passive immunity occurs between mothers and their infants. Immunity is transferred from ***mother to foetus during pregnancy***

a. *Artificially acquired immunity:* When a person is exposed to a causative agent, they can develop artificially acquired immunity. This type of immunity can be acquired through active or passive means.

i. **Artificially acquired active immunity:** When someone receives a vaccine, it boosts their immune system through an injection of the antigen that causes the disease. This process is known as vaccination, inoculation, or immunization. The injected substance is called a vaccine. Examples of vaccines are those for ***pertussis, measles, german measles*** etc.

ii. **Artificially acquired passive immunity**: When someone receives antibodies already made and injected into their body, it's called artificially acquired passive immunity. These antibodies come from someone else's immune system.eg. ***Immunisation for rabies.***

13. **Write a short note on colustrum**

In the initial days of lactation, the breast produces colostrum, a precursor to milk that includes antibodies and white blood cells from the mother's blood. Colostrum is important for providing immunity to the newborn against infections to which the mother is already immune. The antibodies in colostrum help to neutralize harmful bacteria in the baby's digestive system. While breast milk continues to provide antibodies, it is not as concentrated as colostrum.

14. Describe the importance of breast milk or breast feeding

Infection Protection

- Breast milk helps babies stay healthy by protecting them against infections.

Strong Tummies

- Babies fed with breast milk are less likely to get tummy problems.

Fighting Diarrhea

- Breast milk has special things called antibodies that fight common causes of diarrhea in babies.

Perfect Nutrients

- Breast milk gives babies all the right nutrients they need in the perfect amounts.

Guarding Against Illness

- It keeps babies safe from other common illnesses like ear infections and breathing problems.

Heart Health

- Breastfeeding protects against heart problems. Grown-up babies who were breastfed have healthier hearts.
- **Growth Hormones**

- Breast milk has special things that help babies grow strong and healthy.

Smart and Allergy-Protected

- Breast milk makes babies smart and guards them against allergies and diseases like diabetes when they grow up.

15. Define immunization

Immunisation is a process by which a person becomes protected against a disease through an enhancement of their immune response by administering vaccines.

16. Define vaccine

A vaccine is a substance that helps the body build immunity to a specific illness. It usually contains a weakened or dead version of the germ that causes the disease, or its toxins or proteins.

17. Importance of Immunisation

- Vaccines play a crucial role in promoting good health by keeping healthy individuals healthy, which in turn facilitates human development.
- Immunizations have a wide-reaching impact, protecting both individuals and communities.
- Immunizations show prompt effects in preventing and controlling diseases.
- Vaccines are not only lifesaving but also cost-effective solutions.

18. List out the modes of spread of Hepatitis B

Hepatitis B virus is carried in the blood and other body fluids. It spreads in these ways:
Unsafe Injections or Needles:

- If someone uses needles or syringes that are not properly cleaned, the virus can spread.

From Mother to Baby:

- Sometimes, mothers with the virus can pass it to their babies during birth.

Between Children:

- Kids can spread the virus by playing together, especially if there are cuts or scratches.

During Intimate Relationships:

- When people have intimate relationships, the virus can be passed through contact with blood or other body fluids.

Blood Transfusions:

- If someone receives blood from an infected person, they can get the virus through a blood transfusion.

19. Briefly Explain the mode of spread of TB

Tuberculosis (TB) is a disease that can be transmitted from one person to another through the air, usually when an infected person coughs or sneezes. TB can spread quickly in cramped living conditions, areas with limited access to healthcare, and among those who are malnourished. Bovine tuberculosis, a type of TB, can also be transmitted through consuming raw milk from infected cattle.

20. Diseases and affecting body parts

Name of disease - Parts of the body affecting

Hepatitis B - Liver

AIDS - Immune System

TB - Lungs

Poliomyelitis - Nerve cells

Mumps - Salivary glands

Tetanus - Muscles

Pertussis - Respiratory tract

Diphtheria - Throat

CHAPTER VIII

Concern and Issues in Human Development

1. Child labour means forcing a child to work before

(a) 15 years , (b) 14 years, (c) 18 years

Ans. 14 years

2. When an individual deviates from the course of normal social life, his behaviour is called Ans. delinquent

.... is the ability of the eye to see distant objects clearly.

Ans. Visual acuity

3. The visual field is the amount of .... vision.

Ans. side to side

4. A person with .... vision and both eyes working in a coordinated fashion is considered to be normally sighted

Ans. 20'/20'

5. A person is said to be legally blind if his visual acuity is .... or less.

Ans. 20/200

6. .... is the written language for blinds

Ans. Braille

7. A which guides the blind to locate things with sounds.

Ans. Ultrasonic echolocation device

8. A foldable white stick helps the blind to move around freely.

Ans. Hoover cane

9. The degree of hearing loss is indicated in ...., which is a measure of loudness.

Ans. decibels (dB)

10. .... refers to people with hearing loss ranging from mild to severe.

Ans. Hard of hearing

11. The intelligence possessed by a normal individual

Ans.90 and 110 IQ.

12. The formula used to calculate the IQ

Ans. MA /CA x 100

13. Expand AIDS and STD

Ans. Acquired Immunity Deficiency Syndrome

Sexually Transmitted Diseases

14. Name the organism which causes AIDS.

Ans. Human Immuno deficiency Virus or HIV

15. AIDS day is celebrated on

Ans. December 01

16. Syphilis is caused by bacteria known as.................

Ans. Spirochete

2 Mark questions and answers

17. Define child labour

Ans. Child labor involves children under the age of 14 being employed. A child worker is someone under 14 who works to support themselves. Please list the reasons for child labor.

18. Define delinquency

Friedlander defines delinquency as behavior by young people that could be legally addressed. This type of behavior is considered abnormal or anti-social, typically exhibited by individuals who are under a certain age specified by the law. The age range for juveniles can differ among nations, but it often falls between 7 and 16 or 18.

4 Mark questions and answers

19. What are the causes of child labour?

a. Poverty:

- **What Happens?** Kids from poor families often have to work for very little money or sometimes just for food and shelter.
- **Why?** Because their families don't have enough money, and the children end up working long hours.

b. Large Families with Less Money:

- **What Happens?** Families with many kids and not much money find it hard to give them education and other things.
- **Why?** With limited income and many kids, children have to work to help their families.

c. Parents Who Can't Read:

- **What Happens?** Parents who don't know how to read might think children can earn money for them.
- **Why?** Because they believe children can help the family by working, especially when money is low.

d. Kids with No Families:

- **What Happens?** Some kids don't have parents or are left alone for different reasons.
- **Why?** They end up working to have a better life.

e. Laws Not Being Followed:

- **What Happens?** There are rules against child labour, but they are not always followed.
- **Why?** Because even though there are laws, sometimes they are not enforced properly.

20. Explain the causes of juvenile delinquency
The main causes for delinquency are:
a. Not Enough Money:

- When families don't have enough money, kids might not get the chances they need to grow and learn.
- Things like hunger, sickness, and parents not being around make the situation worse, and some kids end up doing things they shouldn't.

b. Families Doing Wrong Things:

- Sometimes, when family members do bad things, kids might follow them and do wrong stuff too.
- Seeing family members doing crimes can make kids think it's okay.

c. Not Getting the Right Help:

- When parents don't give proper guidance and discipline, kids might feel lost and start making bad choices.
- If parents are not consistent or don't care much, kids might not learn how to make good decisions.

d. Home Troubles:

- When families are in trouble or parents are not around, kids might feel upset and do things they shouldn't.
- Problems at home, like fights or being mistreated, can make kids want to leave and do bad things.

e. Hurt by Others:

- Sometimes, kids who are hurt by others might end up doing bad things themselves.
- If they've been abused, they might think it's okay to do harmful things to others.

f. Skipping School:

- When kids don't go to school, they might start doing things they shouldn't just to get by.
- Missing school can lead to bad choices and getting involved in things that are not good.

g. Watching Too Much Violence:

- If kids see a lot of violent stuff on TV or in games, they might think it's normal.
- Seeing violence all the time can make them more likely to act in a mean way.

h. Friends Making Bad Choices:

- When friends do wrong things, kids might join in to feel accepted.
- Wanting to fit in or make quick money can sometimes lead to doing things that are not okay.

i. Not Learning About Growing Up:

- If kids don't learn about growing up in a healthy way, they might get into serious trouble.
- Without the right information, kids might face problems like abuse and not knowing how to act appropriately.

21. Enlist the Characteristic of Juvenile Delinquent children
1. Struggling in school and having trouble learning languages
2. Many students leaving school before completing their education
3. Showing emotional problems and being unresponsive
4. Having difficulty controlling their behavior
5. Engaging in criminal activities such as theft, robbery, and violence
6. Roaming around railroad tracks and streets
7. Experiencing a decrease in cognitive abilities
8. Showing signs of hyperactivity.

22. Briefly explain the characteristics of a child with affected or missing limb

Physical disabilities can cause children to feel inferior, leading to them isolating themselves and exhibiting awkward social behavior.

- As children grow older, they may experience psychological distress as they struggle to meet their aspirations with their abilities.

- Children with missing or affected limbs may show symptoms of anxiety, depression, escapism, and aggression.
- They may also have shorter attention spans, less motivation, and engage in less exploration.
- These children often rely more on adults and have less interaction with their peers, resulting in poor social connections.
- Despite these challenges, the intelligence of orthopedically handicapped children is similar to that of their peers, although they may be less creative.

23. **Write a short note on Snellen chart**

Visual impairment is assessed with the help of the Snellen chart, which was created by Hermann Snellen. This chart is used to measure a person's visual acuity by presenting eight rows of letters in varying sizes. The design of the chart ensures that someone reading it at a distance of 20 feet sees the same as a person with normal vision at 20 feet, also known as 20/20 vision.

24. **List out the characteristics of visually impaired people**

The general characteristics of blind or partially blind people are:

a. Their eyes might appear red, watery, and sensitive to light, blinking more frequently.

b. They often complain of headaches.

c. They tend to hold their head close to reading materials.

d. Their head movements may be noticeable as they lean forward and backward while looking at distant objects.

e. They struggle with social and personal adjustments due to feelings of inferiority.

f. Their mobility is limited.

g. Difficulty in comprehending abstract concepts.

h. They exhibit poor eye-hand coordination.

24. **Explain the main causes of visual impairment**

Visual impairment can result from a variety of causes including congenital and developmental disorders, general diseases, deficiencies, injuries, accidents, and exposure to chemicals.

1. Congenital and Developmental Disorders: These disorders are the primary reasons for visual impairment. They can include conditions where the eyes do not develop fully, abnormally small eye balls, congenital cataracts due to rubella infection, and the presence of a fibrous mesh behind the lens - often caused by the use of oxygen on premature babies in incubators.

2. General Diseases and Deficiencies: Malnutrition, particularly deficiency in vitamins A, B1, B2, C, and D, can also lead to visual impairment. Infections in the mother such as german measles, syphilis, and gonorrhea can also contribute to this condition.

3. Injuries, Accidents, and Chemical Exposure: Various incidents such as injuries, car accidents, head trauma, burns, fireworks, explosions, and workplace hazards can result in blindness. Additionally, consuming toxic substances like methyl alcohol, dyes, and chemicals can also lead to vision issues.

25. Why Some Kids Break Rules:
a. Not Enough Money:

- When families don't have enough money, kids might not get the chances they need to grow and learn.
- Things like hunger, sickness, and parents not being around make the situation worse, and some kids end up doing things they shouldn't.

b. Families Doing Wrong Things:

- Sometimes, when family members do bad things, kids might follow them and do wrong stuff too.
- Seeing family members doing crimes can make kids think it's okay.

c. Not Getting the Right Help:

- When parents don't give proper guidance and discipline, kids might feel lost and start making bad choices.
- If parents are not consistent or don't care much, kids might not learn how to make good decisions.

d. Home Troubles

- When families are in trouble or parents are not around, kids might feel upset and do things they shouldn't.
- Problems at home, like fights or being mistreated, can make kids want to leave and do bad things.

e. Hurt by Others:

- Sometimes, kids who are hurt by others might end up doing bad things themselves.
- If they've been abused, they might think it's okay to do harmful things to others

f. Skipping School:

- When kids don't go to school, they might start doing things they shouldn't just to get by.
- Missing school can lead to bad choices and getting involved in things that are not good

g. Watching Too Much Violence:

- If kids see a lot of violent stuff on TV or in games, they might think it's normal.

- Seeing violence all the time can make them more likely to act in a mean way.

h. Friends Making Bad Choices:

- When friends do wrong things, kids might join in to feel accepted.
- Wanting to fit in or make quick money can sometimes lead to doing things that are not okay.

i. Not Learning About Growing Up:

- If kids don't learn about growing up in a healthy way, they might get into serious trouble.
- Without the right information, kids might face problems like abuse and not knowing how to act appropriately.

26. Why Some People Can't See Well:
a. Problems from Birth:

- Some people are born with eye problems that make it hard for them to see.
- Their eyes might not develop properly, or they could have issues like tiny eyeballs or cataracts because of infections.

b. Sickness and Not Enough Nutrients:

- If someone doesn't eat healthy foods, they might have trouble seeing.
- Lack of vitamins like A, B1, B2, C, and D can cause vision problems. Also, diseases that moms have during pregnancy can affect a baby's eyes.

c. Getting Hurt or Exposed to Dangerous Stuff:

- **Accidents, injuries, and exposure to harmful things can damage eyes and lead to vision issues.**
- From car accidents to burns and chemicals, different things can harm the eyes and cause blindness or other visual problems.
- **So, Some People Can't See Well Because:**
- Their eyes didn't form right from the birth.
- They didn't get the right nutrients from food.

27. Classification of hearing impaired

Hearing loss may be mild, moderate, severe or profound as shown below. It can affect one ear or both ears and leads to difficulty in hearing, conversational speech or loud sounds.

- Mild hearing loss (26-45dB)
- Moderate hearing loss (46-65dB)
- Severe hearing loss (66-90dB)
- Profound hearing loss (greater than 90 dB)

28. Explain the different types of hearing loss

The three main types of hearing loss are as follows:

a. Conductive hearing loss-occurs when there is an obstruction to the conduction of sound through the outer or middle ear, resulting in either blocked sound or a failure to transmit noise through the ear structures.

b. Sensorineural hearing loss-occurs when there is damage to the hair cells within the cochlea, preventing them from sensing fluid movements in the inner ear and therefore not sending signals to the brain.

c. Mixed hearing loss-refers to the presence of both conductive and sensorineural hearing loss in the same ear.

29. Write down the causes of hearing loss and deafness

The causes of hearing loss and deafness can be divided into two viz. Congenital causes and acquired causes.

Congenital causes – There are 2main causes of congenital hearing loss: genetic factors and complications during pregnancy and childbirth. Hereditary and non-hereditary genetic factors can both contribute to hearing loss in newborns. Additionally, certain infections during pregnancy, low birth weight, and birth asphyxia can also lead to hearing loss. Maternal rubella, syphilis, and inappropriate use of drugs during pregnancy are also factors to consider. Severe jaundice in the neonatal period is another potential cause of congenital hearing loss.

b. Acquired causes: Causes that are acquired can result in hearing loss at any point in a person's life. Examples include infections like meningitis, measles, and mumps, ongoing ear infections, buildup of fluid in the ear, head trauma or injuries to the ear, exposure to loud noises, age-related hearing decline, as well as blockages from wax or foreign objects in the ear canal.

30. Write a short note on the different techniques used to aid educational approaches for hearing impaired

i. American Sign Language, also known as ASL, is the primary form of communication used by the deaf community.

ii. Cued speech,-a visual communication strategy, is utilized by some deaf children and their educators or parents. It involves using hand shapes near the mouth to aid in lip reading.

iii. Lip reading - also known as speech reading, involves deciphering the speaker's language by closely observing their facial expressions and movements, specifically their mouth, without the ability to hear their voice.

31. Define mental retardation

The American Association on Intellectual and Developmental Disabilities defines Intellectual Disability as having below-average intellectual functioning, along with challenges in adaptive behavior that are evident from a young age.

32. Write a short note on IQ.

IQ is a meassure of intelligence. The intelligence possessed by a normal individual is said to be between 90 and 110 IQ. The abbreviation IQ stands for intelligence quotient. It is a measure of intelligence. The formula used to calculate the IQ is MA/CA x 100. MA stands for mental age and CA for chronological age. Mentally retarded is children have lower mental age than their chronological age.

33. Explain the classification of mental retardation

World Health Organisation (WHO) gave the following classification of mental retardation.

a. Mild mental retardation IQ 50 – 70

b. Moderate mental retardation IQ 35 – 49

c. Severe mental retardation IQ 20 – 34

d. Profound mental retardation IQ under 20

a. Mild Mental Retardation (IQ 50-70):

- **What is it?** Like calling it "educable," people with mild mental retardation can learn social and communication skills in early years.
- **Skills Level:** By their late teens, they can handle academics at around the sixth-grade level and achieve skills for basic self-support.

b. Moderate Mental Retardation (IQ 35-49):

- **What is it?** Similar to "trainable," individuals with moderate mental retardation acquire communication skills in early childhood.
- **Skills Level:** They benefit from vocational training, can manage personal care with supervision, and adapt well to community settings.

c. Severe Mental Retardation (IQ 20-34):

- **What is it?** This group, about 3-4% of those with mental retardation, struggles with speech development during early childhood.
- **Skills Level:** They learn basic self-care and some pre-academic subjects but might need close supervision for simple tasks in adulthood.

d. Profound Mental Retardation (IQ under 20):

- **What is it?** About 1-2% of people with mental retardation fall into this group, often with identified neurological conditions.
- **Skills Level:** Optimal development happens in a structured environment with constant aid. These individuals need a caregiver's individualized support.

34. Enlist the characteristics of mental retarded children

The general characteristics of mentally retarded children are:

- Slow response time: They take longer to react to conversations and events around them, and sometimes they do not respond at all.
- Lack of clarity: They struggle to communicate their thoughts, needs, and emotions clearly.
- Difficulty learning quickly: They have trouble grasping new concepts as easily as others.
- Trouble understanding quickly: They struggle to comprehend information they see, hear, touch, smell, or taste.
- Indecisiveness: They have difficulty making even small decisions. - Lack of focus: Some individuals with intellectual disabilities have trouble maintaining attention on a person or task.
- Quick temper: Some have difficulty controlling their emotions.
- Forgetfulness: Some individuals struggle to remember information.

35. Briefly explain the causes of mental Retardation

- Some factors that can contribute to mental retardation in children include chromosomal and genetic disorders, maternal infections like rubella or german measles, advanced maternal age, maternal malnutrition during pregnancy, and exposure to radiation.
- Down's syndrome is one of the most well-known chromosomal disorders that can result in mental retardation.
- Additionally, research suggests that older mothers may have a higher likelihood of having children with cognitive impairments.
- It is important for expectant mothers to prioritize their health and well-being during pregnancy to reduce the risk of developmental issues in their child.
- Maternal nutrition: When a mother is malnourished during pregnancy, it can result in both mental and physical defects in the child.
- Radiation: Exposure to radiation during pregnancy has been linked to potential harm to the fetus, leading to various abnormalities such as growth and mental retardation.
- Birth complications: Complications during birth, such as premature or post-mature delivery, prenatal anoxia, or forceps delivery, can lead to brain damage in the child and subsequently cause mental retardation.

- Brain injury and brain diseases: Any head injury or brain diseases that occur during prenatal or postnatal life can result in brain damage and ultimately lead to mental retardation.
- Lead poisoning: Exposure to lead can also contribute to the development of mental retardation.

36. List the preventive measures to mental retardation

- It is important to not have marriages between individuals who are closely related by blood.
- Providing proper prenatal care, including immunizations, a good diet, and medical check-ups, is essential.
- It is recommended that deliveries be attended by a trained professional, ideally in a hospital setting.
- Introducing appropriate weaning foods to babies can significantly reduce the risk of mental retardation.
- Genetic counseling and voluntary birth control are available options for parents to consider, especially for those with chromosomal anomalies. Parents can undergo tests to assess their risk.

37. Explain the mode of spread of AIDS/ Syphilis and Gonorrhoea

- The person who has HIV is capable of transmitting the virus to others. HIV is present in blood and body fluids like saliva, semen, vaginal and cervical secretions, urine, tears, breast milk etc. But it is transmitted from one-person to another only through:
- a. Unsafe sexual contact
- b. Receiving of blood or blood products from infected persons.
- c. Use of non-sterile needles
- d. Sharing of needles among drug users.
- e. From mother to child during birth or through breast feeding

Some of the measures that can be adopted for preventing AIDS and other sexually transmitted diseases are:
- Testing blood for HIV before blood transfusion
- Ensuring the use of disposable needles
- Sterile instrument in hospitals, laboratories, clinics etc
- Control of drug abuse and sharing of needles
- Advocating safe sex and use of condoms etc.
- Awareness programmes to change the attitude and behaviour of the people through mass media, theatre, street play etc.
- Community based intervention among risky population.

****

CHAPTER IX

Resource Management

1 Mark questions and answers

1. Anything useful that helps us in meeting our needs.

Ans. Resources

2. .... is a moral principle or belief that a person holds about some aspect of life.

Ans. Value

3. Define Resources

Resources can be defined as anything useful that helps us in meeting our needs. Resources are what we must possess to get what we want.

3 Mark questions and answers

4. Briefly explain the classification of resources

Resources are classified in to two: human resources and non human resources

Human resources are those resources which are possessed and utilised by individuals. Example: time, energy, knowledge, skills and abilities.

Non-human resources-are external to individuals, but they can be possessed and utilised by them. Example: money, house, land, material goods and community facilities.

5. Resources have certain characteristics. Justify.

i. Resources are valuable: They help meet our needs and desires, which is why they are called resources.

ii. Resources are finite: Every resource has limits. We only have 24 hours in a day. Similarly, our cash salary is fixed. Our energy is also limited. Resources such as water, electricity, and fuel are all in limited supply.

iii. Resources are interconnected: When we work, we rely on resources like time, energy, skills, and equipment. Without enough time and skills, we can't utilize our energy effectively. All these resources work together simultaneously, showing their interconnection.

iv. Resources have alternate uses: Most resources have alternate uses. eg. We can use our family savings for the purchase of a house, equipment or for higher studies. Thus resources have alternate uses.

v. Resources can be substituted: One way to achieve a goal is by substituting resources. For example, we can use our energy and time to walk to school or work, or we can use money to take a bus. Another example is choosing to buy ready-made meals instead of cooking at home. This shows how one resource can be replaced by another.

6. What are the ways of maximizing satisfaction by the use of resources?

The different ways of maximising satisfaction from the use of resources are :

1. Identify all resources that are available.

2. Utilize the appropriate amount of resources.

3. Replace costly resources with more affordable alternatives.

4. Develop habits that promote efficient resource use.

5. Foster practices that boost the accessibility of resources.

6. Embrace sharing resources with others.

7. Preserve and conserve resources by practicing the 3-R's: Reduce, Reuse, and Recycle to optimize satisfaction from their utilization.

7. **Enlist the different steps involved in the management process**

A. Planning B. Organising C. Implementing D. Controlling E. Evaluating

8. **Motivating Factors in Management**

There are three motivating factors in management. These are Values, Standards and Goals

- Values are moral principles or beliefs that individuals hold about various aspects of life, such as honesty, punctuality, kindness, sincerity, health, good habits, and happiness. These are qualities that we strive to adopt and uphold.
- Standards-represent an agreed-upon level of quality. They serve as a benchmark for individuals, prompting them to undertake actions that will result in a desired level of satisfaction. When carrying out any task, we evaluate our performance against a standard. For example, when drawing a diagram, it should be neat and properly labeled, comparable to the one provided in a textbook.
- Goals-are the aims or objectives that individuals strive to accomplish in their lives. They are the targets that we set for ourselves and work towards achieving. Therefore, goals are essential for personal growth and development.

9. **Explain the steps in decision-making**

a. Identifying the problem

b. Obtaining information and formulating a possible courses of action

c. Evaluating the consequences of each alternative

d. Selecting the best possible course of action.

CHAPTER X

Management of Time, Energy, Money and Space

1. An advance plan of activities to be performed in a given period of time.

Ans. Time plan

2. A feeling of extreme physical or mental tiredness is called....................

Ans. Fatigue

3. The stream of goods and services available to a family over a given period of time

Ans. Real income

4. The portion of money income which is kept apart for future contingencies.

Ans. Savings

5. A carefully thought out spending plan of money for the entire family.

Ans. Budget

6. A tentative estimate of a family's income and expenditure over a period of time

Ans. Budget

7. Define Fatigue

Ans. Fatigue can be defined as a feeling of extreme physical or mental tiredness.

2 Mark questions and answers

8. 'Time is a unique human resource'. Justify.

Time is a resource that we all have in equal measure - 24 hours a day. It is crucial to recognize that time is finite and cannot be stretched out. No amount of money can buy more time. We all seem to be constantly racing against the clock. Time is the most discussed topic in everyday conversation. It is essential to allocate time wisely for work, sleep, relaxation, and other commitments.

9. Define time plan

Ans. A time plan can be defined as an advance plan of activities to be performed in a given period of time.

10. Define work simplification

Ans.Simplifying work involves cutting down the time and effort needed for a specific task, ultimately leading to efficient energy utilization.

4 Mark questions and answers

11. Steps in making a time plan

1. List all the activities that need to be done within a certain timeframe. These activities can vary in type.

- Daily activities may include studying, eating, bathing, exercising, playing, etc.

- Weekly activities could involve visiting friends and relatives, going to the library, or watching a movie.

- Seasonal activities might include shopping or attending religious festivals.

2. Identify activities that are time-sensitive, such as school or office schedules.

3. Determine the amount of time needed for each activity and create a rough plan to manage them effectively.

4. Make adjustments to accommodate other weekly and seasonal activities as needed.

5. It's best to group related activities in the time provided in the plan for easier adjustments.

6. Make sure the time plan includes all necessary activities.

7. Monitoring the time plan is crucial for successful plan execution. Regularly check on ongoing activities.

8. Evaluating the time plan after completing tasks within the allotted time is essential to determine its effectiveness.

12. Explain the different types of fatigue - Fatigue has been found to be of two kinds namely physiologicim fatigue and psychological fatigue.

a. **Physiological Fatigue**

In our body, energy is stored as glycogen. When we engage in physical activity, the oxygen we inhale reacts with glycogen to produce energy. This process also leads to the production of waste substances such as lactic acid and carbon dioxide. The build-up of these waste products in the bloodstream results in fatigue. This kind of fatigue is known as Physiological fatigue.

Reasons - Feeling tired can come from various sources like not getting enough sleep, not eating well, feeling stressed from work or home, being out of shape, or having symptoms of an illness.

Ways to reduce physiological fatigue - It's helpful to take short breaks between intense activities in order to reduce fatigue. Resting helps recharge your energy levels and leaves you feeling rejuvenated for further work.

a. **Psychological Fatigue** – Individuals often experience fatigue due to factors such as boredom, frustration, resentment, isolation, pressure, and feelings of uselessness.

Reasons: Boredom may stem from uninteresting, monotonous, or undesirable work and working conditions, resulting in psychological fatigue. Frustration often arises from a lack of job satisfaction and the inability to achieve desired goals, leading to disappointment and stress caused by inexperience, mental concerns, and a lack of motivation and recognition.

Ways to reduce Psychological Fatigue - This can be reduced by keeping the following points in mind.

Making the work engaging and stimulating

Prioritizing time management

- Establishing a well-organized and efficient workspace
- Ensuring proper functioning of work equipment
- Encouraging workers to enhance their skills
- Creating a pleasant and enjoyable work environment
- Setting and achieving small goals to progress towards success
- Allowing free time within the daily work schedule
- Showing appreciation for workers
- Making the work routine feel familiar
- Introducing variety to break up the routine
- Providing periods of rest and relaxation.

13. Explain the different classes of changes in work simplification processes

The different classes of changes involved in work simplification are: Changes in hand and body motions, Changes in work, storage space and equipments used and Changes in end product

A. Changes in Hand and Body Motions

a. Eliminating all Extra Movements

Numerous tasks can be accomplished more efficiently by eliminating unnecessary or redundant movements. For instance, gathering all required materials and tools for a task before commencing work, rather than carrying each item separately, can save both time and effort.

Improving the Sequence of Work

Improving the order and coordination of tasks can save time and effort in a specific job. Sequencing helps make the work easier to manage.

Developing Skill at Work

Skill can be described as the ability to apply acquired knowledge effectively in a practical setting. It is widely believed that regular practice is essential for honing one's skills. This not only reduces the time and effort needed to complete tasks, but also leads to smoother and more efficient work processes. For example, when learning to paint on fabric for the first time, one is likely to expend more time and energy compared to someone who has mastered the art through practice.

Using Correct Body Posture

Maintaining proper body posture is crucial for all activities. Good posture helps conserve energy, while poor posture can lead to decreased efficiency, heightened fatigue, and issues such as back pain. It is essential to consciously practice correct posture when standing, sitting, or bending until it becomes second nature. Additionally, alternating between standing and sitting is preferable to remaining in one position for an extended period of time.

B. Changes in Work, Storage Space and Equipment

This highlights the importance of reorganizing equipment, properly arranging the workspace, providing adequate storage, ensuring that work area dimensions are suitable for the user, and incorporating new, modern tools and equipment. When setting up a workspace, it's crucial to place equipment within easy reach of the worker. The equipment should be easy to handle, grasp, and see to ensure regular and comfortable use. The height of the work area should be tailored to the worker's height, enabling them to store and retrieve items without straining or bending unnecessarily. Utilizing labor-saving devices can also help reduce the time and energy expended in the process.

C. Changes in End Product

The worker may need to adjust certain standards or expectations regarding the appearance, shape, size, etc., of the final product. Each individual holds different standards based on their norms and traditions. Habits can be deeply rooted and challenging to alter. However, it is important to recognize that change is a natural part of life. One should be proactive in embracing new concepts if they can help save time and energy. Thoughtful consideration and effective communication are essential in implementing change. For example, instead of lugging around numerous books for different subjects, one could opt for a modern device.

14. Define family income

Ans. Family income is the stream of resources available to a family such as money, goods and services and the satisfaction the family derives from using these resources over a period of time'

15. What are the different types of family income

Family income can be classified as: Money income, Real income and Psychic income

A. Money Income - Family income refers to the financial resources available to a household from various sources over different timeframes, such as hourly, daily, weekly, monthly, or yearly. This income is typically received in the form of cash and can come from a variety of sources including salaries, bonuses, wages, rental income, profits, gifts of cash, dividends from investments, pensions, lottery winnings, interest earned from bank accounts, and returns on investments.

B. Real Income - Real income is simply the amount of goods and services a family can access over a specific time period. It comes from the family's possessions, skills, and efforts, as well as the community resources available to them.

C. Psychic Income - Psychic income is the feeling of satisfaction that comes from our daily experiences, mostly from how we use our money and resources. It is influenced by how well family members are able to manage their finances and possessions.

16. Types of Real Income

The real income may be direct or indirect.

a. Direct Real Income (Non-Money Income) - Real income is the tangible goods and services used by a family or community without the need for money. For example, by utilizing their own possessions like their house and land, individuals can save on expenses such as rent. Growing vegetables on their property and conducting their own repairs, cleaning, and clothing alterations can also contribute to saving money. Additionally, accessing resources like libraries, parks, and community centers can help increase real income by avoiding unnecessary expenses. For instance, instead of purchasing books, individuals can borrow them from a library.

b. Indirect Real Income - Indirect real income refers to the goods and services that a family obtains through some form of payment, such as money. An example of this would be hiring servants and paying them for their services. Various sources contribute to indirect real income.

1. Goods and services are obtained by exchanging money. For example, electricity, internet, telephone, etc.

2. Fringe benefits include reimbursement for electricity, medical expenses, entertainment bills, free accommodation, transportation, uniforms, subsidized meals, education allowance, etc.

3. Barter system involves exchanging goods directly. For instance, if one person makes jam and another person makes squash, they can trade their products and both benefit from using each other's goods.

17. Importance and Need for Supplementing Family Income

a. Family Goals Achievement - More money income leads to achieving family goals.
b. Inflation - The rise in income doesn't match the rise in prices, leading to the need for additional family income.
c. Future Security - Everyone wants to secure their family's future, with education, unexpected events, and weddings costing a lot.
d. Serving Large Families - To meet the needs of bigger families, supplementing income is crucial for fulfilling all basic needs.

Savings - The portion of money income which is kept apart for future contingencies is known as savings. **Saving = Income - Expenditure**

Importance of Savings

Savings are important for a family due to the following reasons.

1. Economic security

2. Increase in income

3. Restriction on unnecessary expenses

4. Habit of meagre spending

5. Minimising disparity in income and expenditure

6. For fulfilling future needs

7. Helping in implementation of national goals

18. Define family budget

Ans. It is a tentative estimate of a family's income and expenditure over a period of time

19. Enlist the importance of budgeting

1. A financial guide for the family, helping them spend money carefully to avoid exceeding their income.

2. Facilitates the distribution and allocation of income for various expenses, based on their necessity.

3. Encourages cooperation among family members as they work together to plan a budget.

4. Aids in saving money for unexpected emergencies.

5. Identifies unnecessary expenses in a deficit budget, prompting adjustments to maintain balance.

6. Acts as a time log for future needs.

7. Facilitates informed decision-making on budget priorities.

8. Assists in setting financial goals and planning for the future.

20. Guidelines for Making Work Centres More Effective

- Organize work centres in a systematic order to ensure a smooth workflow
- Use clear storage containers with proper labels
- Ensure that all work stations are easily cleanable and maintainable
- Opt for built-in storage solutions like cabinets and cupboards to maximize floor space
- Utilize extra storage areas under stairs, beneath windowsills, and in lofts.

****

CHAPTER XI

Design

1. The three essential aims of good design are order, beauty and ....

Ans. Utility

2. Lightness or darkness of a hue is ....

Ans. Value

3. The brightness or dullness of a hue is ....

Ans. Intensity

4. Find out the principles of design.

a) Movement : .... (Rhythm)

b) Relationship: .... (Proportion)

C) Unity : .... (Harmony)

d) Centre of attraction : .... (Emphasis)

e) Equilibrium : .... (Balance)

5. Define design

Design is defined as any arrangement of line, form, colour, space, value and texture. A good design shows an orderly arrangement of the material used and in addition enhances the beauty and charm of the finished product. The three essential aims of good design are order, beauty and utility.

6. **List out the essential requirements of good structural and decorative design**

When creating a structural design, it is important to consider various criteria:

1. The design should be purposeful and functional.

2. Proportion plays a key role in creating a visually appealing design.

3. The design should complement the material it is made from.

4. Keeping the outline of the design simple is essential.

To ensure a good decorative design, the following guidelines should be followed:

1. Decorations should be used in moderation to avoid overwhelming the design.

2. Place decorations strategically at structural points to enhance the overall shape of the object.

3. Leave enough background space to maintain simplicity and avoid clutter.

4. Ensure that the decoration is suitable for the material being used.

5. The background should complement the pattern being used in the design.

7. Analyse the different types of design

1. Structural design - Structural design, referring to how an object is put together. Every object has a structural design, which includes its size, shape, form, color, and texture.

2. Decorative design - on the other hand, is all about adding decorative elements to the structural design. It's what makes an object visually appealing. Any lines, colors, or materials that are used to enhance the structural design fall under decorative design.

3. Naturalistic design takes inspiration from nature's patterns and elements. Think of designs that mimic mountains, clouds, skies, water, and other natural features.

4. Stylized design -on the other hand, follows a specific artistic style or treatment. It's about creating a design that conforms to a particular aesthetic or artistic approach.

5. Geometric Design: Geometric designs are created using basic shapes such as circles, triangles, and rectangles.

6. Modern or Abstract Design: Abstract art uses form, color, and line to create compositions that may not have clear references to the real world. This type of design is a departure from natural elements, transforming recognizable motifs into non-representational forms.

8. What are the various elements of design

The basic elements of art or design include a. line b. shape and form c. texture d. colour and e. Space.

a. Line: In design, lines play a crucial role in setting the tone and feel of the overall design. They come in various dimensions - length, width, and thickness - that can create different effects. Lines can move vertically, horizontally, diagonally, or in a combination of these directions. There are straight lines, curved lines, and combinations like zigzag, wavy, or scalloped lines. These lines can be thick, thin, long, short, fuzzy, or smooth.

b. Shape and Form: Shape is the general outline of an object, defined by an enclosed line in two dimensions. It can be categorized as geometric shapes (like squares, rectangles, circles, and triangles) or natural shapes (found in nature such as rocks, clouds, and trees). Both types can be observed in nature.

Form is like the three-dimensional version of shape. Just think of the cube, pyramid, and sphere as the three-dimensional versions of the square, triangle, and circle.

c. Texture: Texture refers to the way a material feels when touched or looked at. For example, rough fabric has a coarse texture, while a polished surface is smooth to the touch. Visual texture, on the other hand, is the appearance of a material that can be seen without touching it, like polished stone or woven mats made of coir or jute.

d. Colour: Color is a key aspect of art and design that is received solely through our sense of vision. Our ability to see color is thanks to light. Due to its inherent beauty, color plays a crucial role in the world of art and design.

e. Space: Space in art is often defined as the area that exists between shapes. There are two main types of space in art: actual space and pictorial space. Actual space can be either two-dimensional, like floors and flat surfaces, or three-dimensional, like sculptures, architectural models, or physical objects. Pictorial space refers to the flat surface of the paper, canvas, or other material, also known as the picture plane.

9. Line can create certain emotional effects. Enumerate.

The emotional effect created by lines is as follows.

1. Vertical lines: Vertical lines convey a sense of vitality, liveliness, and elegance. They can be bold, sturdy, and precise in their impact. They create a sense of loftiness. The entrances and curtains in a space contribute to its strength and grandeur.

2. Horizontal lines: Horizontal lines evoke a feeling of calmness, stability, and serenity. They are present in tables, low-backed chairs, and bookshelves, providing a counterbalance to the strictness of vertical lines.

3. Diagonal lines: Diagonal lines represent movement and energy. They disrupt the structure of vertical lines and the solidity of horizontal lines. In residential settings, they are commonly seen in staircases and certain fabrics.

4. Curved lines: When we see curved lines, they give off an air of gracefulness and smooth transition. They bring a sense of elegance, femininity, and adaptability to a design. Curved lines can bring a joyful, subtle, and luxurious touch to any arrangement.

5. Zigzag lines: Zigzag lines are all about creating excitement and energy in a design.

10. **Explain different principles of design**

The following are the principles of design or art.

a. Scale and Proportion

b. Balance

c. Emphasis

d. Rhythm

e. Harmony

a. Scale and Proportion:In art and design, 'scale' is about how big or small an object appears compared to other objects. On the other hand, 'proportion' is all about how the parts of one object relate to each other, or how different objects in a group relate to each other. Proportion can be seen as the ratio of one part to another part, or a part to the whole. That's why some people call proportion the law of relationship.

b. Balance: "Balance in design suggests a sense of equilibrium and rest. It conveys the idea of equal weight on both sides of a central point, achieved by arranging shapes and colors around a center with equal attraction on each side.

c. Emphasis is the principle that directs the eye to the most important element in a composition, guiding it to other details in order of importance."

d. Rhythm: Rhythm is like a smooth road that guides the eye through a design's elements like lines, forms, and colors. It adds a sense of movement that can be created through repeating, changing, spreading out, contrasting, and transitioning.

e. Harmony: Harmony is the key to a successful design. It creates a cohesive and unified feel by organizing consistent elements and ideas. There are six components of harmony: line, shape, size, texture, color, and concept.

11. How can we create emphasis in a design

Emphasis should be laid on few things, non-essentials should be eliminated. Certain areas or objects can be emphasized by

- Grouping objects
- Using contrasts of colour or values
- Using decorations
- Providing sufficient plain background space around objects
- Using unusual lines, shapes or sizes.

12. Analyse the different ways of creating rhythm in a design

"Rhythm can be achieved through repetition, gradation, radiation, opposition, and transition. Repetition is a simple way to create rhythm by repeating elements like color, line, form, or texture. Gradation creates rhythm by gradually increasing or decreasing similar design elements. Radiation makes lines flow outwards from a central point, while opposition forms right angles where lines meet. Transition in rhythm occurs when curved lines guide the eyes from one part of an object to another."

13. Explain the different types of balance

Balance comes in two forms: formal and informal.

Formal balance, also known as symmetrical balance, involves arranging identical objects on each side of a central point. This type of balance is easy to achieve and provides a sense of orderliness, making people feel comfortable.

On the other hand, informal balance, or asymmetrical balance, can be achieved in different ways. For instance, when balancing a heavy object with a light object, the heavier one is placed closer to the center line than the lighter one. Another way to achieve informal balance is by using several smaller objects to balance a single larger object.

14. What do you mean by dimensions of colour. Explain.

Dimensions otherwise known as the properties of colour. There are three properties of colour, namely: hue, value and intensity

a. Hue: Hue is the name of colour such as red, green etc.

b. Value - Value in color theory refers to the lightness or darkness of a hue, which is determined by the amount of white or black added to it. Adding white makes a hue lighter, while adding black makes it darker. However, changing the amount of black or white in a hue doesn't alter the hue itself, but simply lightens or darkens it.

c. Intensity - Intensity, also known as Chroma, describes the strength or saturation of a hue. The purest form of a color, as seen on the color wheel, is the most intense. Intensity can be reduced by mixing grey into the color, which softens its appearance. Another way to decrease intensity is by adding the hue directly opposite on the color wheel.

15. Explain prank colour wheel

Primary colours - As per Prang, all colors can be derived from the three primary or basic colors - yellow, blue, and red. These colors cannot be created by combining other shades.

Secondary or binary colours - When two primary colours are mixed in equal proportions, a binary or secondary colour results.

Red + Blue = Violet

Blue + Yellow = Green

Red + Yellow = Orenge

Intermediate colours- When a primary and a neighbouring binary colour are mixed, the following six intermediate hues are obtained. Examine the following combinations.

Yellow+ green = yellow green

Blue+ green = blue green

Blue+ violet = blue violet

Red+ violet = red violet

Red+ orange = red orange

Yellow+ orange = yellow orange

The three primary hues, the three secondary hues and the six intermediate hues constitute the outer circle in the Prang colour chart. Black, white and grey are neutral colours.

16. Explain colour combinations or colour harmonies

Harmony can be described as the pleasing, well-balanced combination of two or more colors or shades. There are mainly two types of color harmony: harmony of related colors and harmony of opposite or contrasting colors.

Related color harmonies are achieved by using colors that are similar in some way. There are two methods of achieving this:

1. Monochromatic harmony: This involves using only one color and changing its values and intensities. Neutral colors such as black, white, and grey can also be used in this type of harmony.

2. Analogous harmony: Analogous harmony, also known as adjacent colour schemes, utilizes three neighboring colors on the color wheel. This harmony is subtle and practical, utilizing colors of varying intensities and values. For example, a yellow, yellow-orange, and orange analogous harmony.

Contrasting harmonies can be achieved in four ways:

a. Complementary harmony – it uses colors directly opposite each other on the color chart to create a bold contrast.

b. Double complementary harmony – It combines two adjacent colors with their complements for a striking effect. One color should stand out prominently. eg. Blue, orange, blue-violet and yellow orange

c. Split complementary harmony - This is achieved when a primary or intermediate color is paired with the colors adjacent to its complement. For example, combining yellow with red-violet and blue-violet creates split complementary harmony.

d. Triads – These are formed within the Prang color chart by four equilateral triangles. The colors at the points of these triangles make up the triads. The primary triad consists of the three primary colors: yellow, blue, and red. The secondary triad is made up of the secondary colors: green, violet, and orange. Lastly, there are two intermediate triads composed of the intermediate colors: yellow-green, red-orange, and blue-violet.

17. Differentiate warm and cool colours

The colors on the left side of the circle are the warm hues such as red, orange, and yellow. These colors embody the essence of fire or sun, giving off a sense of warmth. They visually appear smaller and shorter, yet they evoke feelings of excitement and happiness. On the other hand, the colors on the right side of the circle are the cool hues like blue, green, and purple. These colors represent vegetation or water, creating a cool and calming sensation. They appear larger and longer, providing a sense of peace and relaxation. Together, the warm and cool colors complement each other, creating a harmonious balance.

18. Illustrate prang colour wheel.

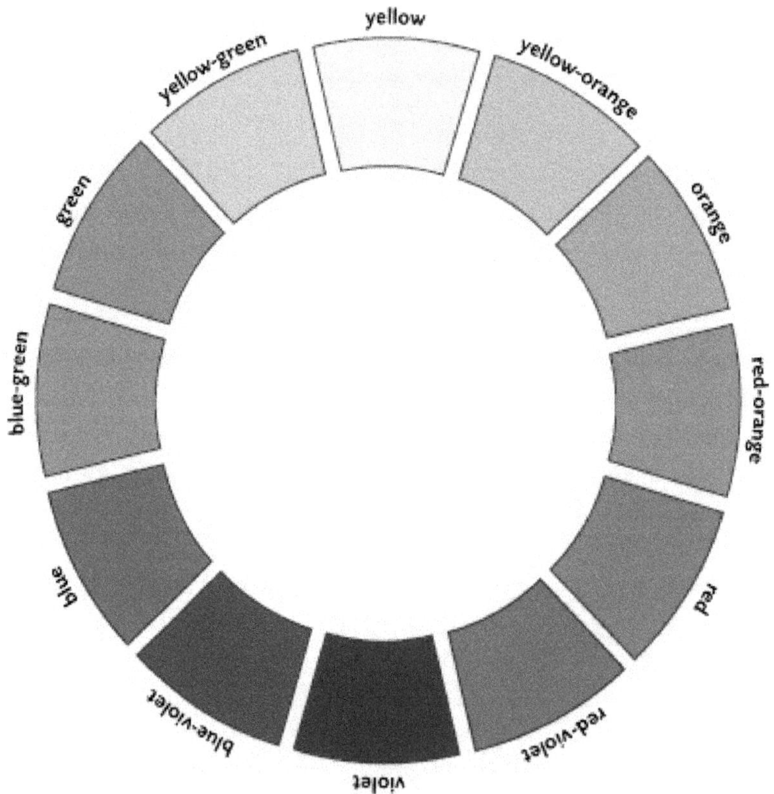

Prang colour wheel

****

CHAPTER XII

Consumer Education

1 Mark questions and answers

1. A .... is an individual who purchases/uses/consumes services/items/products to satisfy wants.

Ans. Consumer

2. Expand the following, FSSAI, COPRA, FPO, ISI, BIS,

FSSAI -The Food Safety and Standards Authority of India (FSSAI)

COPRA – Consumer protection act

FPO – Fruits products order

ISI – Indian Standards Institution

BIS – Bureau of Indian Standards

PFA - Prevention of Food Adulteration Act

3. The enactment of the Consumer Protection Act was on...............

Ans. 1986

4. Define adulteration

Adulteration can be defined as adding extraneous, improper or inferior ingredients to make a product impure.

3 Mark questions and answers

5. List out the importance of consumer education

• Helps to develop the ability to decide and choose things intelligently

• Helps to be alert, well informed and vigilant against corrupt practices in the market

• Helps to take suitable action when faced with a problem

• Helps to demand safe, reliable and good quality products at a reasonable rate

• Helps in optimum utilisation of money and all other resources

6. Write a short note on adulteration

Adulteration refers to the act of adding or taking away substances from a product in order to alter its characteristics, makeup, or overall quality. This can occur either deliberately or accidentally. Deliberate adulteration involves purposely mixing in adulterants to increase profits, while accidental adulteration results from unintentional blending of products during various stages of production, packaging, transportation, or storage. Metal contamination may occur as a result of either deliberate or accidental adulteration.

7. Define consumer aids

Consumer aids are those tools that guide and assist consumers in selecting and buying a product according to their requirement.

8. Write the advantages of Advertisements

- It is a very forceful tool of persuading and influencing the consumer's judgement
- They help the consumer to know and compare various products available in the market
- Help to know the price of the product.

6 Mark questions and answers

9. Analyse the various problems faced by today's consumer.
A. Variation in Prices

- Shopkeepers often markup prices above the Maximum Retail Price to increase profits.
- They sometimes sell unpackaged items without price labels and set prices at will.
- Inferior quality products are sometimes sold at the same price as premium brands.
- Prices can differ between different stores, as expenses like decorations, additional lighting, air conditioning, computerized billing systems, and other overhead costs are factored into pricing.
- Prices are not fixed
- Certain shops spend heavily on advertisements The 'free home delivery' costs are also met by the consumer having to pay more for his/her purchase

B. Defective Weights and Measures

- Use lightweight iron weights that look like the real ones.
- Use measuring jars with false bottoms.
- Use inaccurate weights instead of standard ones. - Use a weighing balance with a wooden beam that tilts when the pans are empty. - Use non-standard weights like bricks and stones. - The pointer on the scale doesn't return to zero when empty. - The balance is missing pointers. - A magnet is placed under one of the pans. - Iron rings are hung on one side of the balance.

C. Hoarding of Commodities
Hoarding is when someone keeps a secret stash of items to make them scarce and drive up prices. It's often seen during times of inflation, war, or uncertainty.
D. Substandard Quality

- Poor quality products are easily available in the market, posing a risk to consumer safety. Additionally, high quality products are scarce even when consumers are willing to pay more.

- Being labeled with a standard mark does not guarantee the quality or safety of a product. Counterfeit items often display fake standard marks, deceiving consumers into thinking they meet certain standards when they do not.
- It is common for store owners and companies to sell inferior products in appealing packaging. Customers are often swayed by the packaging and fail to notice the poor quality of the product, leading to a waste of their money.

E. Inadequate / Misleading Labelling

- Some companies deceive consumers by packaging subpar items in packaging that resembles popular brands, leading to confusion.
- Low-quality products are paired with enticing free gifts and discounts, and consumers may feel pressured to accept free gifts with necessary purchases, such as receiving free bath soap every time detergent is bought.
- Poor quality products may provide false information on their ingredients, storage instructions, and proper usage. Ensure your safety by checking the expiration date before using the product.

F. Customer Persuasion by Shop Keeper

The shopkeeper persuades consumers to purchase a particular product. It demands higher rate of commission for them. A vigilant and sensible consumer should persuade the shopkeeper to get variety so as to select a better product.

G. False Advertisement

There are so many brands in the market that it can be overwhelming for consumers to choose the right one. The products are often marketed in a way that's hard to resist, making consumers eager to buy them. However, the reality may not always match the hype, leaving consumers feeling disappointed when the products don't live up to their advertised quality.

10. Analyse the various standard marks

The standard mark shows that the product meets the quality standards set by the standardizing agency. It also motivates manufacturers to improve competition and enhance the quality of their products on the market.

ISI Mark

The Bureau of Indian Standards (BIS), formerly known as the Indian Standards Institution (ISI), provides manufacturers with the authorization to use the recognized standard mark. This approval is given only after verifying that the manufacturer is skilled and capable of consistently producing products that meet the requirements of BIS. The ISI mark is awarded to a wide range of products including electrical goods, soaps, gas stoves and cylinders, cement, custard powder, common salt, biscuits, baking powder, cocoa, milk powder, condensed milk, wafers, coffee powder, ice cream, chewing gum, drinking chocolate, mineral water, and more.

The AGMARK Standard

The term AGMARK originated from agricultural marketing. The AGMARK standard was established by the Government of India's Directorate of Marketing and Inspection through the Agricultural Products Act in 1973. Its key features include:

1. Categorizing commodities into different grades based on their purity levels, such as 1, 2, 3, 4, extra large, large, medium, small, etc.

2. Specifying the appropriate packaging for various products, such as special egg trays, milk poly bags, oil bags, or cartons.

3. Promoting fair market practices like using standard weights and measures, licensing market operations, and providing mechanisms for resolving disputes.

Fruit Products Order

In 1946, the Government of India introduced a fruit products order, which was revised in 1955. This order is overseen by the food and nutrition board of the Ministry of Food Processing Industries. Its key features include setting minimum quality standards for preserved foods made from fruits and vegetables, guidelines for hygiene and sanitation, maintaining standards throughout the production process, packaging and labelling instructions, and regulating the temperature of food containers. The agricultural marketing advisor has the authority to issue licenses for manufacturing fruit and vegetable products, with the FPO mark indicating compliance with the order.

c. ECO Mark: The BIS has recently introduced these marks, which serve as a testament to the ISI standard of the product and also help with recycling and pollution control. This mark can be found on products such as paper bags, jute bags, plastic goods, and packing materials.

d. Wool Mark: The International Wool Secretariat awards this mark to guarantee that products bearing it are made of pure wool. Alternatively, the label must specify the percentage of wool and other fibers used in the final product.

e. Silk Mark: This mark is awarded by the Indian Silk Organisation. This mark ensures that the product has been made of pure silk.

f. 100% vegetarian mark: This mark ensures that all the ingredients in the product are 100% vegetarian. The green dot symbol identifies vegetarian food and the brown dot symbol identifies non- vegetarian food. It is applicable for packaged food products.

11. What are labels? Write the advantages of labels

Label informs the consumer about the quality and method of its usage. Label is engraved, printed or pasted on the packing of the product. Bureau of Indian Standards has fixed certain standard for a complete label. A good label must provide the following information.

i. Name of the product

ii. Brand name

iii. Trade mark

iv. Manufacturer's name and address

v. Name of country in which product made

vi. Contents / ingredients

vii. Net weight / volume / length

viii. Instruction for use

ix. MRP (Maximum Retail Price)

x. Warnings and precautions

xi. Directions for use, care, maintenance, storage

xii. Date of manufacture and expiry.

Advantages of Labels

- Labels are useful for helping consumers make informed decisions about products.
- Ingredient lists, particularly for food and medicine, can be beneficial for individuals with allergies.
- Standard marks indicate the quality of a product.
- Labels assist in identifying, comparing, and checking prices and quantities.
- Contact information for consumer complaints is typically provided on labels.
- Labels offer guidance on product storage and usage.
- Special promotions such as discounts or gifts are often featured on labels.

12. List out the advantages of packing

a. It enhances the appeal of the product.

b. It prevents spoilage by protecting the contents from contamination, damage, or evaporation.

c. It is resistant to breakage.

d. It ensures that there is no risk of adulteration.

e. It eliminates the possibility of pilferage.

f. It is convenient to carry.

g. It helps indicate the quality of the product through standardized markings.

13. Explain the Salient Features of Consumer Protection Act

- This act applies to both goods and services. Goods are produced by manufacturers and purchased by consumers from manufacturers or sellers. Services can include transportation, electricity, water, roads, and more.
- Consumer redressal forums exist to address complaints from consumers about products or services from companies, firms, sellers, or shops. These forums handle issues such as misspelling, unsatisfactory service, repairs, guarantees, defective products, accidents, and damage from unsafe products. Their decisions are legally binding for product and service providers.
- Under Consumer Protection Act, three judicial systems have been set up to provide relief to consumers. In this system, consumer forums have been set up at various levels which are functioning to safe guard the interests of consumers. Under this system, many forums and commissions have been set up at various levels where consumers

can lodge their complaints.

i. In each district, there is a Consumer Dispute Redressal forum that is overseen by a judge equivalent to a Session Judge. The judge is supported by two other members. This forum handles cases where compensation is up to 20 lakh.

ii. At the state level, there is a State Consumer Dispute Redressal Commission headed by a judge equivalent to a High Court Judge. Like the district forum, this commission also has two members assisting the judge. Here, cases involving compensation ranging from 20 lakh to one crore are heard.

iii. The National Consumer Dispute Redressal Commission, led by a Supreme Court Judge and four members, handles cases involving compensation exceeding one crore. Appeals against State Commission orders fall under the jurisdiction of the National Commission, with the Supreme Court serving as the ultimate decision-making body.

According to this law, complaints must be resolved within 3 months or 5 months if lab testing is required. Clause VI of the Consumer Protection Act outlines consumer rights, and there is no fee for filing a complaint, ensuring even the less privileged can seek justice.

14. How to File a Complaint via consumer redressal forms?

- You can file a complaint in person or by registered mail.
- Make sure to fill out the complaint form completely.
- The defendant must be notified of the complaint via registered mail.
- Give the defendant 15 days to respond or make amends.
- Attach documents like bills, receipts, and warranty cards to prove the validity of the complaint.
- The complaint form should include all details of the complaint, the loss suffered, and the compensation requested.
- Submit three copies of the complaint with relevant documents to the consumer forum or commission.
- An affidavit along with complaint should be submitted wherein it should be specifically stated that the contents of the complaint are true and correct and accompanying documents are true and duly attested.

****

Abbreviations

- CARE - Cooperative for American Relief Everywhere
- FAO - Food and Agricultural Organization
- UNICEF - United Nations International Children's Emergency Fund
- ECCE - Early Childhood Care and Education
- ICDS - Integrated Child Development Services
- AIDS - Acquired Immuno Deficiency Syndrome
- HIV - Human Immuno deficiency Virus
- ELISA - Eenzyme-Linked Immuno Sorbent Assay (test to detect AIDS)
- MMR - Mums, Measles, Rubella
- DPT - Diphtheria, Pertusis, Tetanus
- BCG - Bacille Calmette-Guerin
- TB - Tuberculosis
- DOTS - Directly Observed Therapy Short Course (Treatment for TB)
- FPO - Fruits Product Order
- Agmark - Agricultural Marketing
- FSSAI - Food Safety and Services Authority of India
- COPRA - Consumer Protection Act

Matching Terms

- Eating disorders – Anorexia Nervosa, Bulimia nervosa, obesity
- Hereditary disorders - Haemophilia, Gout, Myopia, Down Syndrome, Muscular dystrophy, Diabetes, Phenyl Ketonuria, Sickle cell anaemia
- Sexually Transmitted Diseases - AIDS, Syphilis, Gonorrhoea
- Elements of design - Line, shape, form, colour, texture, space
- Principles of Design - Harmony (unity), proportion (relationship), balance (equilibrium), rhythm (movement), emphasis (centre of attraction)
- Budget - Tentative plan of expenditure
- savings - Income – Expenditure (for future contingencies)
- Time plan - Plan of activities to be done
- Fatigue - Feeling of extreme tiredness
- Self esteem - Ones feelings
- Self Concept - Ones own qualities and competence
- Hearing impaired - American sign language, Cued speech, Lip reading
- Visually impaired - Braille,
- Cooing - Explosive vowel like sound
- Babbling - Inarticulate meaningless words

IMPORTANT YEARS

- FPO - 1955
- COPRA - 1986

Childhood Diseases

Name of Disease	Organism	Causative organism	Vaccine	Mode of spread
Diphtheria	Bacteria	Coryne Bacterium Diphtheria	DPT	Air droplets via cough, cold saliva
Pertussis	Bacteria	Bordetella Pertussis	DPT	Air droplets
Tetanus	Bacteria	Clostridium Tetani	DPT	Infected when gets in contact with contaminated objects through wounds. deep puncture wounds caused by dirt nails, knives, tools, wood splinters and animal bites.
DPT - Diphtheria, Pertussis, Tetanus				
Mumps	Virus		MMR	Air droplets
Measles	Virus		MMR	Air droplets
Rubella	Virus	Mother to fetus	MMR	Air droplets
MMR- Mumps, Measles, Rubella				
Poliomyelitis (Crippling Disease)	Virus		OPV (Oral Polio Vaccine)	From infected water directly in to wound
Tuberculosis	Bacteria	Mycobacterium Tuberculosis	BCG (Within 72 hours after delivery Pentavalent	Air droplets Treatment - DOTS
Hepatitis -B	Virus	Hepatitis B Affecting Liver	Pentavalent	Direct contact Same for all sexually transmitted disease

Childhood diseases